Welsh
Wildlife

David Jones

First impression: 2003
Copyright © David Jones and Y Lolfa Cyf., 2003

Cover design: Ceri Jones
Cover photograph: Snowdon Lily by Llyr Gruffydd, Red Squirrel by Michael Evans, Red Kite by the author

ISBN: 0 86243 654 0

Printed on acid-free and partly recycled paper
and published and bound in Wales by
Y Lolfa Cyf., Talybont, Ceredigion SY24 5AP
e-mail ylolfa@ylolfa.com
website www.ylolfa.com
tel (01970) 832 304
fax 832 782

Acknowledgements

The author and publishers would like to thank the following individuals and organizations for their assistance in the production of *Welsh Wildlife*:

Anne Bunker, Eileen & Michael Evans, John Evans, Lefi Gruffudd, Rebecca Gwynne, Vicky Harrison, Russel Hobson, Kay Jenkins, Rhys D. W. Jones, Owain A. S. Jones, Piers Langhelt, David Remucal, Tim Rich, Alan Roderick, Craig Shuttleworth

Butterfly Conservation, Caerphilly Library, Cardigan Bay Forum, Countryside Council for Wales, Greenland Whitefronted Goose Study Group, Greenpeace, National Museum of Wales, Mammal Society, Newport Library, Royal Society for the Protection of Birds, Tenby Museum, Vincent Wildlife Trust, Whale & Dolphin Conservation Society

Picture Credits

GWGSG – page 49; Michael Evans – front cover, pages 51, 53, 55, 69, 74; Scott Hand – page 22; David Jones – front cover, pages 14, 51, 58, 66, 93, 94; Natural History Museum – page 97; Tenby Museum – page 25.

Contents

Introduction

Gwinllan a roddwyd i'n gofal yw Cymru fy ngwlad,
I'w thraddodi i'm plant,
Ac i blant fy mhlant,
Yn dreftadaeth dragwyddol…

(A vineyard entrusted to us is Wales, my country,
To be handed down to my children,
And to my children's children,
A heritage for ever…)

Saunders Lewis

For a country of its size, only some 20,763 square kilometres, Wales has an extraordinary diversity of habitats. From Yr Wyddfa in the north to the Gwent Levels in the south, including all points east and west, the landscape of the principality provides a rich variety of natural habitat of considerable wildlife value. Three National Parks, five Areas of Outstanding Natural Beauty (AONBs), 58 National Nature Reserves (NNRs) and more than 1,000 Sites of Special Scientific Interest (SSSIs) are all testament to an outstandingly beautiful and diverse Welsh countryside. The importance of the marine environment of Wales, too, cannot be over-stated. Skomer Island, situated off the Pembrokeshire coast, for instance, is one of only three national marine nature (NMRs) reserves in the UK and much of the Welsh mainland coastline has been designated as of European importance.

The countryside of Wales and the rich tapestry of flora and fauna that are an inextricable part of it should be considered as much a part of our national heritage as any of the treasures that are housed in our museums and art galleries. The pages that follow give but a brief account of that heritage and of fifty of the principality's most celebrated wildlife species. A complete treatise on the subject was never the intended format and, indeed, as famed natural historian William Condry says in his inspirational volume *The Natural History of Wales*: "The natural history of even so small a country as Wales is inexhaustible in its scope and a whole encyclopedia on the subject could still leave a good deal unsaid."

Sadly, the complex beauty of the Welsh landscape has been under attack in the last fifty years. Man's maximal machine power and minimal consideration for the world about him, have inevitably led to a profoundly impoverished landscape. The disappearance of thousands of kilometres of hedgerows, around ninety per cent of traditional hay meadows and large tracts of heath and fenland within the principality are just a part of the price paid for high-profit-yielding modern agriculture. The all consuming plough has often left an expanse of undistinguished farmland which, as far as wildlife is concerned, is almost sterile. In the past, the belief has somehow come about that such ravages will not irrevocably damage the very fabric of the natural beauty of the countryside, that all is reparable. It must be now evident that this is not the case. Cynics would suggest that the battle for the countryside has already been lost, that the conservation movement is merely locked in a last desperate struggle to retain something, anything, from a landscape torn apart. Thankfully, this is not the generally accepted wisdom. It is, though, a truism that the fate of the countryside and the future of the wildlife of Wales do not lie in a few reserves, but in man's attitude of mind. And it is clear that if this attitude does not radically alter to one of comprehending the serious situation before us, it will sadly soon become a case of things that once were... but are no more.

David Jones
March 2003

FLOWERS

According to the *New Atlas of British and Irish Flora* of 2002, there are more than 2,100 flowering plants to be found in Wales. The diverse nature of the Welsh countryside has resulted in a rich and varied flora that includes many rare and endangered species. Many plants found within Wales occur only rarely elsewhere and others such as a Black Mountain Hawkweed (*Hieracium tavense*), Tenby Sea Lavender (*Limonium transwillianum*), Wild Cotoneaster (*Cotoneaster cambricus*), Snowdonia Hawkweed *(Hieracium snowdoniense)*, Trelleck Bramble (*Rubus trelleckensis*), Snowdon Eyebright (*Euphrasia rivularis*), and South Stack Fleawort (*Tephroseris integrifolia maritima*) are endemic species.

Unfortunately, the last century has seen the disappearance of nineteen species of British wild plants and whilst this represents less than one per cent of the British flora, another 51 species, including a number confined in range to Wales, are on the very brink of extinction. Such a state of affairs has been brought about due to a number of factors. At every turn, modern intensive farming and forestry have resulted in the erosion of habitats and the disappearance of species of wildflowers, both common and rare, before our very eyes. The loss within the principality of nine tenths of hay meadow habitat, some of which may have existed since medieval times and often supported over a hundred species of wildflowers, is the end result of the inexorable march of modern agriculture.

Yet, not all the blame for the reduction in plant numbers can readily be attributed to commercial concerns. Many species now considered to be rare have often become so as a result of over-collecting. T. W. Barker, in his *Handbook to the Natural History of Carmarthenshire* of 1903, showed considerable foresight with regard to conservation, in stating: "There is, however, a drawback connected with this increase of interest – the danger lest some new-fledged naturalists, in their zeal to obtain specimens of some rare species, may perhaps unwittingly succeed in exterminating it." The thoughtless practice of specimen collecting was most prevalent in Victorian times and the list of species that have suffered from such predation makes sad reading. Take for instance the example of the Snowdon Lily. It is now considered so rare as to warrant inclusion on a list of species most at risk. Whilst the plant has never been regarded as common, botanist J. E. Griffith reported it being carried away in large numbers from its native Welsh hillside in the 1880s. A similar sad tale can be told of the gross exploitation by commercial horticulturists of the Tenby Daffodil. Once a common sight in the pastures around Tenby, the species was mercilessly plundered, so that by the turn of the century few wild specimens remained. And such acts of wanton destruction of native populations are not confined to the dim and distant past. As recently as the late 1970s, a foreign professor of botany was seen carrying off a basketful of the rare Sea Lavender (*Limonium paradoxum*) from its only British mainland site, at St. David's Head.

Many plants, although on the very edge of extinction in Wales or even Britain, may in fact be widespread on mainland Europe, and therefore their possible loss to us may be considered by some not to be serious. The reasoning of such a school of thought might well be that the disappearance of such species in Wales, whilst regrettable, would not mean a complete loss to the world and thus extinction in the truest sense of the world. However, wild flowers, like other wildlife, act as a barometer by which can be judged the state of the environment as a whole. In addition to this, should such an indifferent attitude prevail, once the species most at risk disappear, how long after will it be before the widespread and common meet a similar fate? Indeed, many species of wild flowers formerly considered to be common are already increasingly becoming less abundant. Take for example the Cowslip (*Primula veris*), a flower that in the past was picked by the armful by children throughout Wales. Whilst it would not be accurate to describe it as rare, it is certainly not witnessed in such profusion, nor in as many localities as in the past.

In the county of Radnorshire alone, 46 species of wildflower are believed to have become extinct since the nineteenth century, and a similar story could perhaps be told of every Welsh county. The list of extinctions include Cottonweed (*Otanthus maritimus*), formerly found at Caernarvonshire and Anglesey but lost and gone forever in the 1890s; Purple Spurge (*Euphorbia peplis*), last seen at Aberystwyth in 1805; Irish Saxifrage (*Saxifraga rosacea*), formerly found at a sole British site in Caernarvonshire but thought to have become extinct around 1960; and Downy Hemp Nettle (*Galeopsis segetum*), last recorded at Bangor in 1975.

On a happier note, there have been some remarkable recent discoveries. Take for instance the first records for Wales of Welsh Groundsel at Ffrith in 1948, Radnor Lily at Stanner Rocks in 1975, Viper's Grass (*Scozonera humilis*) at Cefn Cribwr and Early Gentian (*Gentinalla anglica*) at South Pembrokeshire in 1996 and the amazing 're-discovery' of the Snowdonia Hawkweed at Cwm Idwal in 2002.

As we move into the 21st century, safeguarding Wales's precious flora must be placed high on the national agenda. For, as natural history author James Robertson states: "How much longer Wales will remain a land of flowers is open to question. If it can do so, the cultural and economic benefits in the long term will be great."

Fen Orchid *(Liparis loeselii ovata)*

Counted amongst the rarest of flowering plants in the Welsh flora is a small, visually unremarkable yet distinguished wildflower named the Fen Orchid (*Liparis loeselii*). A few duneland sites in Wales are the home to around 95% of the entire British population and the principality could, perhaps, lay claim to being the European stronghold of this endangered little green orchid.

A member of the Orchidaceae family of plants, *Liparis loeselii* is a short perennial which attains a height of around 6–20 cm. Its yellow-green flowers, which appear around June-July, are somewhat anonymous compared with the showy blooms of exotic species, or even most British orchids. Known in Welsh as *Gefell-lys y fignen*, the plants found in Wales have been classified as a separate sub-species from *Liparis loeselii* because of its shorter size and a noticeable broadness in the leaves compared to specimens from other locations.

The plant was first discovered in Wales in Carmathenshire by R. Browne in 1897. The find was recorded by renowned botanist J. W. Barker, who wrote: "In July 1897 a friend of mine, Mr R. Browne, brought me several plants which he had picked up on the Burrows near Pembrey. Amongst them were two plants of a little green orchis, which were quite new to me. I found to my surprise they were Liparis… " Later, Barker followed up the find by visiting Carmarthenshire personally: "On the 22nd of June, 1899, I walked out to the valley, where to my delight I found 15 to 20 plants of it scattered about." Unfortunately, within a decade of its discovery, the Pembrey site had been wiped out.

The plant has had something of a chequered history in Wales where it has been recorded at around half a dozen wet, calcareous, dune slack sites. It was recorded as recently as 1972 at Oxwich Burrows, in 1975 at Crymlyn Burrows, and in 1982 at Pendine Burrows, but is now believed to have disappeared from all three places. It has also gone from Baglan, Margam and Tywyn Burrows. At the latter site, during the 1950s, it was reported by respected lady botanist Mrs I. M. Vaughan as being plentiful, but, sadly, the last recorded sighting there was almost 30 years ago. Today, the species appears to be confined to two south Wales sites – on dunes at Kenfig, and Whiteford National Nature Reserves in Glamorgan.

The latter station gives a clue to the exacting environmental conditions required for the plant to flourish. During the Second World War, when south Wales sites were used for tank manoeuvres, the artificially created instability of the dune systems saw populations of the Fen Orchid increase. With the heavy artillery of man gone and the outbreak of myxomatosis in the fifties, which wiped out large rabbit populations that kept competing species in check, the orchid has had a hard time of it. Without continual wind-blown sand movement and grazing, rank vegetation takes over, creating unsuitable conditions and effectively eradicating the plant.

In 1994, a project to improve the habitat for the Fen Orchid was undertaken at Kenfig Dunes National Nature Reserve in Glamorgan. The project involved mowing and removal of competing vegetation from the slacks. Results have proved very satisfactory, with new plants being recorded from at least one project site. Work goes on to try and ascertain the extent of over-stabilised dune sites, including surveys to establish any unrecorded remnant pockets of the species and research into ways the dune habitats can generally be better managed. There is also the possibility of re-establishing populations at sites where the plant has become extinct.

The Fen Orchid can be regarded as something of a sentinel species, giving an indication of the general well-being, or otherwise, of the fragile dune system environment. As a spokesman for the Countryside Council of Wales has said: "The orchid is a key species. If we lose the Fen Orchid, we also stand to lose a whole tapestry of plants and insects."

Newport Centaury *(Centaurium scilloides)*

Located on a windswept, grassy seacliff on the Pembrokeshire coast and recorded at only two other sites in Britain, the Perennial, or Newport Centaury (*Centaurium scilloides*), is undoubtedly one of Wales's botanical treasures. A very rare member of the Gentian family of flowers, it is a semi-prostrate perennial with roundish leaves. Its large, five petalled pink flowers, 15–20 mm in diameter on a single stem, distinguish it from the smaller, clustered blossoms of the more widespread annual, the Common Centaury (*Centaurium erythraea*). *C. scilloides* flowers are usually seen in bloom amongst dense turf in north Pembrokeshire during July–August. In Britain, besides its Welsh location, where it is at its most northerly European latitude, it is found at only two other places, both in west Cornwall.

The plant was discovered at its Welsh cliff top site as recently as 1918. However, there seems to have been some confusion over who actually first found the plant at Newport. In 1950, for instance, F. Lillian Rees, in her *A List of Pembrokeshire Plants,* recorded it as being, "First discovered by Mr T. B. Rhys of Tenby,

1918." Mention has also been made of famous botanist George Claridge Druce as being the discoverer. Druce himself, though, took no credit and, indeed, recorded Tenby botanist J. Arnett as being the first to discover it "At Newport, Pembroke," in June, 1918. It does seem that the latter has the best claim to the record. There were also doubts at the time that the plant may

have been deliberately introduced by the hand of man. Druce was to write: "The question arises – is the new *Centaurium* native?" His doubts were based on the fact that it had been found at no other location in Britain, although he did consider: "It might well be found in the Channel Islands and north Devon or Cornwall." Despite all the reservations in botanical circles at the time, the plant was to prove native and Druce's belief that it might be found in Cornwall well-founded. Since its discovery almost eighty years ago, the Newport colony has continued to flourish and increase in size. A somewhat distinguished plant, because of its local distribution in Wales it has come to be known in the principality as the 'Newport Centaury', and such is the beauty and rarity of *Centaurium scilloides*, it could equally lay claim to the title of 'The Pride of Newport'.

Radnor Lily *(Gagea bohemica)*

It is hardly credible that a species of plant could go totally un-observed and thus unrecorded by the legions of botanists that have scoured the Welsh landscape for new species during the last three hundred years. Yet this is exactly what happened until forty years ago, when a single specimen of *Gagea bohemica* was first discovered in Britain at an isolated rocky site in Wales.

A member of the Liliaceae family, the plant is a bulbous perennial with bright yellow flowers and very narrow leaves. Although widespread throughout Europe and Western Asia, the species had never been recorded anywhere in Britain. In April 1965, following a field trip to Stanner Rocks, an outcrop of igneous rock set in the Radnorshire countryside, eminent botanist R. F. O. Kemp noticed a small white flower amongst specimens of moss he had collected. After careful identification of the bloom, Kemp concluded it must be a new record for the rare Snowdon Lily. For a decade the Stanner *Lloydia* record stood, until one of the best kept secrets in the history of British botany was finally revealed.

April 1974 saw the visit of R. G. Woods of the Nature Conservancy Council to Stanner Rocks. There he came upon a single white flower similar to the one found by Kemp, amongst hundreds of non-flowering plants. Woods compared this specimen with a photograph taken by Kemp of his specimen. Both were identical but, unlike the Snowdon Lily, were somewhat hairy. In January 1975, Woods paid another visit to the Stanner site. There he found a single plant in bloom bearing flowers which, although similar, were bright yellow in colour and not white. A further visit in February the same year finally solved the puzzle, when he noted that the same flower had turned white. It was clear that when the blossom was past its best and fading, it lost its yellow colouration. Further inspection showed that the plant undoubtedly belonged to the genus *Gagea*, although it was evident it was not the Yellow Star of Bethlehem *(Gagea lutea)*, which up until then was the only member of the family to be recorded in Britain. Two experts were called upon to give their opinion and, with the available evidence, came to the conclusion that the species must be *Gagea bohemica*. Such a judgement caused a sensation as the species had never before been recorded in Britain. To this day, Stanner Rocks remains the sole British site of the beautiful golden *Gagea bohemica*, later christened the Radnor Lily, to mark the location of the remarkable find.

Rock Cinquefoil *(Potentilla rupestris)*

Of all the native flowering plants on the Welsh flora, there are few whose existence in the principality can be considered as precarious as that of the Rock Cinquefoil. Always regarded as something of a botanist's prize, it has in recent times been recorded at only four sites in the whole of Britain. Two of these stations are located in Wales but their foothold here remains so tenuous that even with careful protection, extinction still remains a very real possibility. A member of the Rose family, *Potentilla rupestris* is an erect perennial that grows to a height of 20–50 cm. Unlike most cinquefoils, whose blooms are yellow, its flowers, which appear in May–June, are pure white, closely resembling those of the wild strawberry. Home to the very rare plant in Wales is on igneous rocks at Craig Breidden, Montgomeryshire, and on the upper reaches of the River Wye, below Builth Wells in Radnorshire.

It was first discovered in Britain by celebrated Welsh botanist Edward Lhwyd at "Craig Wreidhin, Montis Gomerici" – Craig Breidden, Montgomeryshire – around 1689. The plant was to remain relatively plentiful at Craig Breidden for some time after Lhwyd's initial discovery. Reverend W. W. How, for instance, when describing the botanical delights of Craig Breidden in *The Phytologist* in 1859, was to comment: "To the botanist the Breidden is an unrivalled mine of wealth… as he clings for support to some tuft of herbage above, he suddenly finds in his hand a bunch of leaves which he has not seen before, and which he soon finds out belongs to the Breidden plant, *Potentilla rupestris*, unknown elsewhere but happily plentiful here and growing where it is not likely to suffer greatly from the ravages of unprincipled collectors. " However, suffer it did, for less than two decades later, Dr James Cosmo Melvill, a botanist whose name is most closely linked with the flora of Breidden Hill, was to report that the plant had become scarce there. And, by the turn of the century, due to the unwelcome attentions of Victorian plant collectors, there were believed to be more specimens of the plant in the vicarage garden at Criggion than on its native Breidden. The following 30 years saw a continual decline in numbers so that eventually, the plant was reported as being extinct on the hill. However, just when botanists had resigned themselves to the loss, the plant was 're-discovered' in 1940, when "a few" plants were found to still exist.

Having survived the ravages of plant collectors, the 1954 designation of the Breidden Hills as a Site of Special Scientific Interest seemed to offer some measure of protection. A decade later, though, the status of *P. rupestris* was again giving conservationists serious cause for concern. At one stage it was thought only a single plant was known with certainty to exist, although after further extensive searches, three more plants were located. After considering the desperate plight of the plant, a group of keen naturalists decided to take action to try and safeguard the colony. Following well laid plans, seedlings from original Breidden stock were reared in controlled conditions and then transplanted onto the site. Unfortunately, due to a number of factors, most prominent of which was the encroachment by a nearby forestry plantation, the experiment was only a partial success. Today, the future of the Breidden colony, which according to a Nature Conservancy Council survey in 1987 amounts to just seven plants, remains as uncertain as ever.

The history of *Potentilla rupestris* in Radnorshire is less well documented and altogether more confusing than that of the Breidden colony. It is known for certain that the plant was discovered in the county by the Reverend Augustin Ley, on 13 August, 1886. Ley told of finding around fifty plants "occupying the side and summit of a range of rocks of the Llandeilo series in the south-west of the county." Because of the then persistent dangers from plant collectors Ley was not too specific about identifying the exact location of his find. However, R. G. Woods, author of the 1993 *Flora of Radnorshire*, states: "There are good reasons to believe Ley found it in the site on rocks in the flood zone of the Wye." There, due to seasonal flooding, the future of the plant is as insecure as it is on Breidden Hill.

Snowdonia Hawkweed *(Hieracium snowdoniense)*

In 2002, there was great excitement in botanical circles when it was revealed that a wildflower last seen almost half a century earlier and long regarded as lost to Wales was found again in the principality. The Snowdonia Hawkweed has never been a common plant. It was first discovered in 1892 by distinguished Caernarvonshire botanist J. E. Griffith whilst he was writing his book *The Flora of Anglesey and Caernarvonshire* (1895). The plant, which grows to a height of about 30 cm, has a rosette of green leaves, a long stem and a cluster of beautiful golden-yellow flowers. One distinctive feature is that the backs of the flowers and stalks are covered in black, glandular hairs. A plant of impeccable Welsh pedigree, *Hieracium snowdoniense* has in total been recorded from seven mountain ledges in Snowdonia and nowhere else in the world.

Just over sixty years after Griffith's initial discovery, the plant was recorded for the last time when hawkweed expert Peter Sell reported seeing it, whilst he was hanging from a rope at Cwm Idwal in 1953. Despite numerous widespread searches by a legion of botanists, the plant had not been seen since and was presumed extinct. In 2000, botanists turned detective and again went in search of the elusive plant. Using historical data and details of specimens in the Welsh National Herbarium and other scientific collections, the history and distribution of the plant were pieced together. The information was used to target searches of the mountains but, after several exhaustive and exhausting expeditions, no plants were found. It appeared that the Snowdonia Hawkweed was indeed extinct.

Undaunted, in 2002, four dedicated botanists undertook another expedition to Snowdonia, and their perseverance paid off when they rediscovered a single plant in full flower. Some scientists concluded that the plant had been pushed to the very brink of

extinction by the huge increase in sheep grazing at high altitudes in the mountains over the last fifty years. Most hawkweeds are highly palatable to sheep, and it is probable that the rare plant had been literally eaten to extinction in all but the remaining single site. Seeds were collected from the Cwm

Idwal plant and sent for cultivation to the National Botanic Garden of Wales. Director of the garden, Professor Charles Stirton, said of the rediscovery: "We often hear of extinctions in the tropical rainforest and other parts of the world but we have a very unique flora in these parts. We don't have a vast number of species, but many of what we do have are restricted to mountain tops and are very, very rare."

The Snowdonia Hawkweed certainly comes into that category, for with only one solitary plant known for certain to exist, it is one of the rarest wildflower species in the world. It is, for example, infinitely rarer than the celebrated Snowdon Lily, of which there are seven sites with hundreds of plants in Wales alone and a range that extends across Europe and North America.

Snowdon Lily *(Lloydia serotina)*

One of the most celebrated species in the entire Welsh flora has to be the Snowdon Lily. An alpine-arctic wildflower of mystery and unassuming beauty, it is undoubtedly one of the natural treasures of Wales. It was discovered around 1688 by seventeenth century Welsh botanist Edward Lhwyd, who reported that it grew on The Glyders and various cliffs on Snowdon. A plant of singular charm, it has a single crocus-like bloom with six white, purple-veined petals which is usually seen in late May

or early June. The leaves are very slender, almost thread-like, hence the alternative Welsh names *Y Bryfedog* – the spiderwort or *Brwynddail y Mynydd* – rushed-leaved mountain plant. Thought never to seed in Wales, it spreads slowly by forming new bulbs alongside the main plant. Its range is confined to rock ledges at between 1,500–2,500 feet in the lime- rich cliffs of Snowdonia and just why the plant never survived in England and Scotland remains something of a mystery. However, the nearest site to Snowdonia where it is found flowering is in the Alps, some 700 miles away. Perhaps the greatest discovery of all the fifty or so species recorded by Lhwyd in Wales, an early reference to the plant is made by fellow botanist Dr Richard Richardson, who wrote: "Mr Lhwyd show'd me [the plant] in flower on the side of Trigfylchau towards Nant-phrancon, the flower is large for the size of the plant something resembling that of Luzula." However, it was not until after Lhwyd's death in 1709, that the Snowdon Lily was named in Latin by R. A. Salisbury *Lloydia Serotina* in his honour (Lloyd being the anglicised version of Lhwyd).

Following its discovery, the plant became the focus of all botanists who came to Wales and for some it became an obsession. It is recorded, for instance, that eighteenth century botanist Sir Thomas Gage almost lost his life in Snowdonia whilst climbing in search of the elusive *Lloydia serotina*. Undoubtedly, the plant has suffered from the unwelcome attentions of unscrupulous plant collectors. In the recent past, the plant was recorded at twelve locations in Snowdonia but now, due to such depredations, it is only found at seven.

Referred to as the 'Glory of Snowdonia', *Lloydia serotina* has long had a special status in Wales, which was further underlined when the crown of the 1991 National Eisteddfod had a representation of the iconic flower incorporated into its design.

Tenby Daffodil (*Narcissus pseudonarcissus obvallaris*)

Although the daffodil is known throughout the world as Wales's emblematic flower, there is, in fact, a separate species of the flower that can lay claim to the title of the true Welsh daffodil. The Tenby Daffodil is a distinct, dwarf, early flowering member of the narcissus family. A flower of some mystery, the origins of the smooth textured, uniformly brilliant yellow *Narcissus pseudonarcissus obvallaris* are uncertain.

Down the centuries, scientific theory and colourful legend have vied with each other to account for the flower's inexplicable appearance and limited range within west Wales. The unlikeliest but, nevertheless, the most charming explanation dates back to the time of the Phoenicians. It tells how a ship from the fleet of the ancient seafaring race, following a regular trade route, was blown off course and sought shelter at Saundersfoot. There, the Phoenician captain was intrigued to see natives cooking over fires fuelled by anthracite. Realising the potential of the fossil fuel, he returned the following year to barter a cargo of daffodil bulbs for it. Perhaps an altogether more plausible explanation tells that the introduction of the flower was at the hands of medieval French or Italian monks. Certainly, many religious houses were founded in Pembrokeshire and, maybe, monks brought the plant with them for both ornamental and herbalist purposes. A further, altogether less romantic theory may possibly provide the answer to the origin of the flower. This suggests that it is a descendant of a variety introduced into the area that accidentally hybridised, flourished in local soil and weather conditions and eventually became the dominant species. Yet, even this theory does not provide a totally satisfactory answer and perhaps its true origins will forever remain shrouded by the mists of time.

Up to the beginning of the nineteenth century the Tenby Daffodil was witnessed in profusion in the fields around the town from which it took its name. However, the increasing horticultural trade of the time saw truck loads of the bulbs lifted and transported to London for sale at Covent Garden. One report of the time said: "…As a rule, the farmers on whose land they grew regarded them as little better than weeds and readily parted with them for a trifle and sometimes for nothing…" Finally, so great did the predation become that, by the turn of the century, few wild specimens remained. Today, as a legacy of the past, the Tenby Daffodil is regarded as all but extinct in the wild. It does, however, continue to survive, albeit as a cultivated bloom, and can be seen on roadsides and embankments of its native west Wales.

Tintern Spurge *(Euphorbia serrulata)*

The Upright Spurge is an enigmatic wildflower from the south-east corner of Wales that periodically appears in great numbers, yet remains an extremely rare plant. A member of the Euphorbiaceae family of plants, it is similar to the Broad-leaved Spurge (*Euphorbia platyphyllos*) but appears more delicate. An annual, it has long, partially toothed leaves and yellow flowers which bloom June–September. It is generally found on carboniferous limestone woodland clearings and quarries in the Lower Wye Valley and, elsewhere in Britain, just across the border, on similar habitat, in western Gloucestershire.

Also known as the Tintern Spurge, it was discovered around the picturesque village in Gwent in 1773 by Reverend John Lightfoot. His diary of Tuesday, June 29, 1773, records the find: "By the brookside, going down from the abbey to the forge where they make wires". Later reference is made to the species by Charles Cardale Babbington (1808–1895), Professor of Botany at Cambridge University, who made frequent trips to Monmouthshire during the years 1834–1876. He recalls that it was: "plentiful from above Tintern down the river for several miles."

Although a very rare plant, within its locality, when major upheavals of soil have taken place, such as road widening schemes, it quickly colonises freshly turned soil and is witnessed in profusion. Yellow drifts of the flowers have in the past even been witnessed along the main road to Tintern. In 1997, one colony of plants at St. Briavels in the lower Wye Valley rose from around 50 plants to an estimated 1,600 after having vehicles driven over the site. A spokesman for Forest Enterprise said: "The spurge likes disturbed ground. As luck would have it, we had contractors harvesting on the site and we asked them to put as much traffic as possible over the areas where the spurge had grown." The site was then left, allowing the plants to grow and flower and the remarkable increase in numbers was witnessed.

Recent estimates put the entire population within the Wye Valley at no more than ten small colonies, and why its range remains so restricted remains a mystery. It is, however, believed that its overall decline in numbers can be attributed in part to the replanting of native woodland with conifers, since the plant appears to flourish in areas of good light.

Welsh Groundsel *(Senecio cambrensis)*

Most plant discoveries in Wales were made in a period that commenced in the seventeenth century and spanned three hundred years. Then, botanists scoured the landscape in the hope of laying claim to being the discoverer of a species new to Britain. However, as recently as forty years ago, a species not only previously unrecorded in Britain but also new to science was discovered on a roadside in Flintshire.

Despite its name, Oxford Ragwort (*Senecio squalidus*) is not native to Britain but originated on the lava slopes of Mount Etna in Sicily, Southern Italy. It first arrived in Britain in 1794, when it was introduced to Oxford Botanical Garden. Another common weed found throughout Britain is the Groundsel (*Senecio vulgaris*), familiar to most people as a supplementary food for pet budgerigars. Some time, at an unknown date, Oxford Ragwort and Groundsel crossed. Generally such hybrids are sterile; however, in this case the result was a fertile, recognisably different plant, in effect a new species. On 15th August, 1948, Horace Edgar Green discovered the newly formed species at Ffrith in Flintshire. Later, in 1955, Green's find was confirmed and named *Senecio cambrensis* by Effie M. Rosser. Rosser noted that amongst the differences of the species from either parent plant were the larger seeds and pollen with four pores instead of three. A curious twist in the tale occurred in 1957, when a previously unrecognized specimen of Welsh Groundsel was discovered in a herbarium in Oxford. Collected by H. Humphrey Jones from a site at Brynteg, Denbighshire, in 1925, it pre-dates Green's discovery by more than two decades.

Ten years after its first discovery at Ffrith, the plant was also recorded at Queensferry and, by the late 1960s, had been found at Colwyn Bay. There are now believed to be around 35 sites, of which four contain more than a hundred individual plants.

Welsh Poppy *(Meconopsis cambrica)*

As well as the familiar cornfield variety, Wales has its very own species of poppy. The Welsh Poppy, which has a bright yellow rather than a scarlet flower, is a true native of the principality. Known in Welsh as *Pabi Cymreig*, the somewhat symbolic Welsh flower has a widespread distribution; it has been recorded in thirteen Welsh counties. It was first discovered on the mountains of north Wales by London herbalist and apothecary Thomas Johnson in 1639. Shortly afterwards, fellow botanist John Parkinson made mention of it, describing it as: "the yellow bastard poppy of Wales". Amongst the earliest records is reference to it being found: "in many places of Wales in the valleys and fields at the foote of hils and by water sides, about a mile from a small village called Abbar, at the midway from Denbigh to Guider, the house of a worthy gentleman Sir John Guin as also neere a wooden bridge that giveth passage over the river Dee to a small village called Balam which is in North Wales…" One piece of folklore that grew up, specifically about *Meconopsis cambrica*, was that it flourished best on Welsh soil. There seems little evidence of this and, indeed, the species appears to do well in the whole of its range, which includes the English counties of Yorkshire, Somerset, Devon and Cornwall.

Wild Cotoneaster *(Cotoneaster cambricus)*

Described in 1800 as 'The Botanical Garden of Cambria', the massive carboniferous limestone headland of the Great Orme today still retains an interesting and varied flora. Around four hundred species of flowers, trees and shrubs have been recorded there but the jewel in the crown of the Orme's plants is undoubtedly the Wild Cotoneaster.

A member of the Rosaceae family of plants, the Wild Cotoneaster is known as the 'Great Orme Berry' because of its red globular berries. A small deciduous shrub with pale pink flowers and oval leaves, which are green above and grey and woolly beneath, it is believed to have been introduced from the Continent by a clerical community which settled on the Great Orme in 1284. First discovered by John Wynne Griffith of Garn in 1783, it was not until 1821 that the record was confirmed by English botanist William Wilson. At the time of its discovery it was considered to be reasonably plentiful on the Orme, which was and still is its sole British site. Because of its rarity, the plant attracted the unwelcome attentions of unscrupulous plant collectors and this, together with over-grazing by sheep and feral goats, led to the belief early this century that the species had become extinct. However, against all odds, half a dozen plants managed to survive.

In 1970, it was apparent that this miserable colony had, over the previous two decades, shown little sign of regeneration and the species as a whole in Britain faced almost certain extinction. Alarmed at such a prospect, dedicated conservationist M. Morris embarked upon a series of experiments in an effort to save the species. Firstly, cuttings were taken and placed in a compost mixture. These failed to root. Undaunted, in 1973, Morris decided to air layer the undermost branch of one of the wild plants. This proved more successful and within twelve months Morris had a new

Cotoneaster plant. In 1977, he took five cuttings and tried a new rooting medium. By spring the following year all had successfully taken. Morris's efforts continued and included growth from seeds and even force-feeding seeds to pigeon to discover if passage through the digestive tract of birds was a requirement for successful germination. The summer of 1979 saw the climax of Morris's dedication when, with the assistance of a member of the Llandudno Cliff Rescue Team in finding suitable sites, seven cotoneaster plants were planted out on the Great Orme.

In February 1908, Willoughby Gardner, vice president of the Llandudno Field Club, made a plea to "save *Cotoneaster vulgaris [cambricus]* from extinction in Great Britain". It was his cherished hope that the species: "might once more be firmly established in its one British habitat before it may be too late and it is gone forever." Current numbers are put at 33 plants – there were 34 but disaster struck when one was accidentally destroyed by an over-zealous, well intentioned conservation worker, who was actually trying to aid the cotoneaster cause by clearing ground cover.

Yellow Whitlow Grass *(Draba aizoides)*
Renowned for its unspoilt beaches and rugged coastline, the Gower Peninsula on the south-west coast of Wales is also home to a rich and varied flora. Perhaps the rarest and most important of all Gower plants is a small, tufted perennial known as Yellow Whitlow Grass, which is found on carboniferous limestone cliffs there and nowhere else in Britain.

Known in Welsh as *Llysiau Melyn y Bystwn*, the Yellow Whitlow Grass looks like a typical rock garden plant with its rosette-like cluster of dark green leaves. Flower buds often appear in December and the four petalled bright yellow blooms can open as early as February. A resilient little plant, it is unaffected by short periods of drought or frost and can sometimes be seen flowering during March snowstorms. In his book *Wildlife, My Life*, celebrated naturalist William Condry tells of his first sighting of *Draba aizoides* in 1958 during such conditions. Inclement weather had almost forced him to abandon his field trip in search of the plant but he persevered until a heavy shower of driving wet snow sent him scurrying for cover. It was whilst sheltering under overhanging rocks that suddenly: "a patch of bright yellow caught my eye. And that was how, with snow falling thickly about me, I first saw the Yellow Whitlow Grass." He added: "I remember with affection my first meeting with this beautiful little plant that adorned the snow covered sea-cliffs of Gower that day…"

Generally, the most likely time to see the plant in full flower is the third week of March. However, dependent on location, it can be at its best at the end of April and in places like the shaded areas of the south-western cliffs at Pennard, flowering may be as late as May. Around 90% of mature plants flower each year but the setting of seed is often inhibited by grazing snails. A distinctive feature of the plant following flowering is the formation of silvery 'penny' seed cases. Individual plants tend to last for around ten years during which time they attain a diameter of 12 cm and a height of 6 cm.

The plant was first discovered in 1795 by John Lucas the younger, a member of the Swansea gentry, and recorded in Sowerby's *English Botany* of 1804 as growing "near Worms Head". An early record, from 1803, was made by W. Turton who recorded it: "growing wild abundantly on walls and rocks" at perhaps its most famous of locations, on Pennard Castle. A further nineteenth century sighting was recorded at Worms Head in 1887, by the entirely appropriately named botanist T. B. Flower. In the past, doubts had been expressed about *Draba aizoides*' status as a truly native plant. Claims were made that its appearance in Wales was due to the hand of man; there is, however, no evidence of such artificial introduction. It is found growing naturally in rock crevices on south facing, dry, sunny cliffs and rock faces along a 17 km stretch of South Gower coastline, stretching from its place of discovery to Pwll Du Head, where it was first recorded in 1904. Why the plant is confined in Britain to the Gower Peninsula remains a mystery. The nearest other localities are on mainland Europe, on the Belgian Ardennes and the Côte d'Or near Dijon, where it is often referred to as the 'hunger flower', presumably because of the barren soils on which it appears to flourish.

Past ravages by unthinking gardeners and collectors resulted in it disappearing from the most accessible locations on Pennard Castle and Southgate cliffs. Today, a more enlightened attitude has seen it flourishing and even spreading within its local range. If threats from spring grazing by sheep and accidental trampling by man are kept in check, the future of Gower's 'golden grass' seems to be assured.

FERNS

Found growing in almost every region throughout the world, ferns are amongst the most primitive and ancient of plants. Of the estimated 6,000 species, some of which are believed to date back to around 400 million years ago, only forty or so are found in Wales. Included amongst these are a Welsh variety of the Southern Polypody and two ferns considered to be amongst the rarest and most endangered species in Britain.

The history of ferns in Wales has not been an altogether happy one. The Victorian craze of fern collecting, or pteridomania, saw a number of species suffering at the hands of collectors, who were often referred to as 'Botany Bens'. The rarer ferns were mercilessly exploited. Collectors used a piece of equipment called a radiator, which was basically a hook on the end of a long pole, often twenty feet long, which was used to dislodge rare ferns from inaccessible sites. Famed botanist Samuel Brewer is recorded as using one to collect specimens of the extremely rare Alpine Woodsia in 1726. Commenting on the predation of the times C. C. Babbington wrote: "extirpation is the rule in Wales with tourists and collectors who call themselves botanists". He concluded that the rarest of fern species were: "subject to constant solicitations from botanical tourists".

From the earliest of times, Wales was thought to be home to its own species of fern. Known as Welsh Polypody (*Polypodium cambricum*), it was first recorded in Ray's *Synopsis* of 1690, where it was described as growing "on a rock in a wood near Dennys Powis castle". It was thought to be a distinct separate species but was later discovered to be a variety of the Southern Polypody (*Polypodium australe*). Undoubtedly the rarest of ferns, found not only in Wales but throughout Britain, are Alpine and Oblong Woodsia. Both are so scarce that they are given the protection of law under the Wildlife and Countryside Act, 1981.

Alpine Woodsia *(Woodsia alpina)*

It is thought possible that Alpine Woodsia is a hybrid of Oblong Woodsia (*Woodsia ilvensis*) and a species not found in Britain *Woodsia glabella.* Similar to the Oblong Woodsia, its fronds, which are 3–15 cm long, are more delicate, less scaly and less deeply lobed. The generic name of both this species and the Oblong Woodsia is in honour of famed eighteenth century botanist Joseph Woods. Found in damp rock fissures in Caernarvonshire, the species has been heavily preyed upon in the past by collectors. Samuel Brewer recorded, that on 17 August, 1727, he found at Snowdon for the first time the rare fern: "which was first observed by Mr Green on a high, rough rock that standeth perpendicular and faceth the head of the lake called Llyn-Cwm-y-Ffynnon, 'tis about the middle of Glogwyn-y-Garnedd, and the said rock is as high as it is hardly possible for a man to climb up to: it grew very much exposed to view, and hardly any grew lower than ten feet, so that we were forced to take them down with a twenty foot pole with a radicator at its end." One of the earliest descriptions of the fern is given by James Bolton in his *Filices Britanniae* of 1785, perhaps the first book on British ferns. Bolton's specimens were obtained from Snowdon.

Holly Fern (*Polystichum lonchitis*)

So named because it superficially resembles the Christmas evergeen, the fronds of the Holly Fern, although appearing prickly, are actually leathery and quite soft to the touch. Commonly, the glossy, dark green leaves grow to 15–30 cm but at lower altitudes, in damp shady spots, they can achieve greater luxuriance and a height of up to 60 cm. New frond growth usually begins in May but unfurling generally does not take place completely until June-July. An arctic–alpine species, in Wales, where it is at its southern-most limit in Britain, it is confined to crevices on mountain crags in Caernarvonshire.

It was first discovered there by Welsh botanist Edward Lhwyd on perhaps his earliest of trips to Snowdon, on 24 August, 1682. His find was later recorded in the first edition of John Ray's *Synopsis* of 1690 as growing on "Clogwyn y Garnedh y Crib Goch Trygyvylcha". Fellow botanist Dr Richard Richardson, who often accompanied Lhwyd in his explorations of Snowdonia, recorded a find of the Holly Fern: "in the moist rocks which face Grib Goch directly opposite to a fountain almost at the middle of the rock

(where by Mr Lhwyd's assistance in climbing the rock I got several plants of it). It is half a mile from the highest part of the mountain in a steep horrid black rock to the west and nowhere else that I know of to be found… " Following Lhwyd's discovery, botanists from all over Britain traversed Welsh mountain crags in search of the plant. Inevitably perhaps, the quest for the elusive fern over such treacherous terrain had tragic consequences. At least one life was lost, that of botanical guide William Williams who fell to his death at Clogwyn y Garnedd in 1861 whilst, it is said, in pursuit of *Polystichum lonchitis.*

In the nineteenth century the species came under threat from collectors and so great were their predations that its disappearance from Wales became a real possibility. True botanists, like J. E. Griffith, became alarmed at the extent of the collecting. In 1894, he was to record: "This fern is disappearing fast and I am afraid it will soon become extinct." Thankfully, the Victorian fern collecting craze did not last and a number of Welsh *Polystichum lonchitis* which grew in the most inaccessible of sites escaped the predation.

Killarney Fern (*Trichomanes speciosum*)

Once the most coveted of all Welsh ferns, Killarney Fern was first discovered in Snowdonia by J. F. Rowbotham in 1863. The delicate, filmy fern, that has fronds 7–35 cm long, is generally found at sites offering humid, shady conditions, often near waterfalls. In Wales, it has been recorded in recent times at sites in Cardiganshire, Merionethshire and Caernarvonshire. Manchester botanist Rowbotham told of discovering it: "in a large hole formed by fallen rocks alongside a cascade of water…" He added that the colony, said to be the finest in Britain, was growing: "in the form of a beautiful curtain, down which the water is constantly trickling; the whole having much the appearance of a crystal screen". Such a description must have had pteridophiles from all over Britain heading for Wales but the location of the find was kept secret and has since not been rediscovered. This has added to the romance and legend of the fern in Wales and has led countless botanists to question if the colony still exists and is just waiting to be found.

One colony that does still exist is that discovered by Welsh school master John Lloyd Williams in 1887. He discovered it on Moel Hebog, near Beddgelert, and despite suffering sorely at the hands of an unprincipled collector shortly afterwards, the colony recovered and has continued to survive. However, half of the eight colonies known in Victorian times have been plundered and are today no longer in existence. Today there are believed to be seven small populations of the celebrated fern to be found in Wales.

Oblong Woodsia (*Woodsia ilvensis*)

Found in Caernarvonshire on damp, alpine rock crevices at altitudes between 1,200–2,500 feet, Oblong Woodsia was first recorded by Edward Llwyd in 1690 at Clogwyn y Garnedh. Similar to Alpine Woodsia, it is a less delicate fern with fronds 5–15 cm long and hairy, scaly stems. Never a common fern, historically perhaps its best known location was at the entrance of a disused asbestos mine.

It has been suggested that both Oblong and Alpine Woodsia are relict populations in long term decline. If this is indeed the case, then, undoubtedly, their decline has been hastened by the attentions of unscrupulous collectors. For instance, a colony on Glyder Fawr was completely destroyed by collectors in 1844, and the species was once recorded in Merionethshire but has long since disappeared from there.

TREES

Today, Wales is a land of trees again. The total land area covered by trees is some 13.8%. This figure is equal to that of around 600 years ago and is a massive increase on the 3% figure recorded in 1871. Unfortunately, 47.9% of that current tree count is made up of less wildlife-friendly coniferous plantation which often produces a green but monotonous landscape and sterile undergrowth. The most common conifer species found in Wales is the Sitka Spruce (*Picea sitchensis*), a tree that in terms of being a wildlife haven, hardly bears comparison with the main broad-leaved tree, the Oak. One survey on the richness of insect life of broadleaf and conifer forestry starkly illustrates this. Since insects form the bottom line of the food chain, the number of species present can often give an indication of the potential as a wildlife habitat. The results of the survey showed, that on a mature lowland oak, in excess of 300 species were present. In contrast, the insect species on a Douglas Fir (*Pseudotsuga menziesii*) numbered less than twenty. Despite the current conifer imbalance things are improving. The area of broad-leaved woodland has increased since 1980 and relative proportions of broadleaves to conifer have gone up from 29% to 44%. Clearly, it is essential that a balanced approach to future woodland management is maintained. As a far-sighted report by the Countryside Commission in 1987 said: "Forestry should be a multi-purpose activity with the aim not only of producing timber but of improving the landscape, creating wildlife habitats and more and better recreation sites."

Undoubtedly, the specialities of the Welsh landscape are the

Sorbus variety of trees. The English Whitebeam (*Sorbus anglica*) for instance, with an entire British population of around 600, finds a home in the principality, as does *Sorbus eminens* which numbers only 250. Even rarer is the appropriately named Welsh Whitebeam (*Sorbus leptophylla*) which numbers just 44 and is confined to two carboniferous limestone sites in Powys. In the early 1990s, the world of botany was rocked by the discovery in Wales of the True Service Tree (*Sorbus domesticus*), a species thought to have been extinct in Britain since 1862. Two colonies of the rare tree were discovered on limestone cliffs running from Barry to Southerndown. Remarkably, one specimen was estimated to be four hundred years old.

Lesser Whitebeam *(Sorbus minima)*

The whitebeam is a tree of singular beauty. The oval leaves of the tree are green on the upper surface and white below. When viewed on a native hillside on a sunny breezy day, the brilliant whiteness of the undersides of the leaves flash in contrast with the rich green upper parts. This creates an almost kaleidoscopic effect. It is a variable tree in the wild, with a number of related forms with restricted ranges. In Wales, within the Brecon Beacons National Park, there exist three species that are unique. *Sorbus minima*, the Lesser Whitebeam, was first discovered by a cleric in 1893 at Craig-y-Cilau. This limestone escarpment forms the northern edge of Mynydd Llangattwg, near Crickhowell, Breconshire. Reverend Augustin Ley spent most of his life as curate and, later, vicar of St. Tysylio's Church, Sellack, near Ross-on-Wye. He was, however, also a botanist of some note, discovering many plants new to Wales and a few new to science. In the *Journal of Botany* of 1895 he was to report: "In 1893 I found a *Pyrus* (*Sorbus*) in Breconshire... location on a limestone mountain cliff called Craig Cille, near Crickhowell;

also on limestone rocks at Blaen Onnen, two miles westward from Craig Cille. Undoubtedly native and in great abundance at the former station."

Few plants could ever lay claim to be of sufficient importance to be discussed at the House of Commons. However, in 1947, Alderman Tudor Watkins, M.P. for Brecon and Radnor, warned that the unique tree, discovered by Ley over fifty years earlier, was in grave danger from British Army mortar practice. Remarkably, after further discussion,
Mr Bellenger, the then Secretary for War, ordered the army to pull out of the area. Today, the entire world population of the tree that stopped an army is put at around three hundred.

Ley's Whitebeam (*Sorbus leyana*)

After his death, Ley's work was recognised when, in his honour, another rare species of whitebeam discovered in Breconshire was named *Sorbus leyana*. Thought to have derived from Mountain Ash (*Sorbus aucuparia*) and Rock Whitebeam (*Sorbus rupicola*), Ley's Whitebeam flowers in late May–early June and fruits in September. The entire world population, which probably numbers no more than sixteen native trees, is confined to carboniferous limestone cliffs at Penmoelallt Woodland Reserve and Darren Fach Nature Reserve on the southern edge of the Brecon Beacons National Park. In addition, of six nursery grown saplings planted by the Forestry Commission in 1962, four have survived. In 2002, one specimen, planted at the Forest Enterprise Garw Nant Visitor Centre, was nominated by the Tree Council as one of Britain's 'fifty great trees for fifty great years', to mark the Golden Jubilee of Queen Elizabeth II. Currently, the future of Ley's Whitebeam appears secure. However, a threat on the horizon could be a proposed re-opening of the Dan y Darren quarry. Should this go ahead, dust emissions would undoubtedly pose a threat to what is, internationally, one of Britain's rarest plants.

BIRDS

Since records began, no fewer than 419 different bird species have been noted in Wales. Of that number, perhaps 185 are regularly witnessed and fewer still have bred in the principality. Yet Wales, once the last refuge in Britain for the magnificent Red Kite, is today still home to significant populations of birdlife. For instance, the importance of Welsh islands to British, European and, indeed, international bird populations cannot be overstated – Skomer is home to 10,000 Puffin, the largest colony in Southern Britain; Grassholm is the second largest gannetry in the world, with 100,000 birds; Skokholm has a population of 35,000 Manx Shearwaters (*Puffinus puffinus*) and with Skomer holds around 50% of the entire world population of the seabird.

Like elsewhere in Britain, overall, the landscape in Wales has become profoundly impoverished by modern agricultural methods. This has seen once common birds become endangered species. The decline in species like the Skylark (*Alauda arvensis*), Dunnock (*Prunella modularis*) and even the Song Thrush (*Turdus philomelos*) has been nothing less than catastrophic. The Tree Sparrow (*Passer montanus*), once a widespread and familiar bird, has been particularly hard hit. Populations in Wales have fallen 90% in the last 25 years and current numbers are put at less than 2,000 pairs. The Curlew (*Numenius arquata*), once a common sight on farmland across the length and breadth of Wales, has also suffered a massive decline since the 1960s. Numbers of the once familiar wader have now reached an all time low with only 4,000 breeding pairs remaining in the principality. Another victim of less than sympathetic agricultural practices has been the Lapwing. It is a salutary lesson when a once common farmland bird such as the 'peewit' should, in the matter of a few decades, be transformed into a Candidate Red Data Species. Yet that is exactly what has happened, and one report published in 2001 concluded that: "there is a direct link between population declines of once common birds and indicators of agricultural intensification, including cereal and milk yields and the number of tractors per farm worker." Estimates of the effects such farming policies have had put the loss in Wales as millions of common farmland and woodland species during the period 1972–96.

Yet it is not all bad news. The saving of the Red Kite and its soaring numbers shows exactly what can be achieved where there is a will. The ongoing efforts to save species such as the Black Grouse and Lapwing also seem likely to succeed, given time. Then, there are the amazing recent new breeding records in Wales. The current number of breeding species in the principality is around 150 and now included in the list are the Hoopoe (*Upupa epops*), which first nested in Montgomeryshire in 1996; Eider Duck (*Somateria mollissima*), which bred on Puffin Island in 1997; and the Dartford Warbler (*Sylvia undata*), with two new records, in Gwent in 1997 and on the Gower in 1998. Whether these records are, as some scientists claim, attributable to climate change due to global warming and are a precursor of things to come remains to be seen.

Black Grouse (*Tetrao tetrix*)

A once familiar feature of heather moorlands in Wales, the spectacular Black Grouse has been in decline in the last three decades and is today one of Wales's most endangered birds. The male is a striking bird with black plumage and white wing bars. At close quarters, the distinctive bright red wattle over the eye and lyre-shaped tail become apparent. By contrast, the more secretive female is a smaller, brown bird. The spectacle of male birds lekking or displaying is a sight not easily forgotten. Males perform the ritual at traditional communal leks throughout the year but most commonly between March and June. When lekking, cock birds emit a characteristic cooing, bubbling 'song'.

During the nineteenth century, although only considered a minor game bird, significant numbers fell victim to the guns of man. Indeed, on one Carmarthenshire estate alone, on average, 168 birds were shot each year between 1888 and 1895. During the first three decades of the twentieth century numbers remained reasonably stable but after the War and for a period into the 1970s a significant increase in numbers was witnessed. This was almost certainly due to the establishment of new conifer plantations which, because they were fenced off from grazing livestock, at first allowed heather to flourish. However, once the conifers matured, the heather was shaded out. As a consequence, from the mid-1970s, grouse numbers began to tumble. Mature conifer plantations and soaring numbers of grazing sheep are two main causes of the loss of heather. Heavily grazed land dramatically reduces both cover and food for grouse chicks. Indeed, it can produce 25% fewer caterpillars – the preferred diet of grouse chicks – than heather does.

During the 1980s numbers of male birds in Wales seriously declined. From 264 at around ninety leks in 1986, numbers fell to only 131 during the following decade. Typical of the situation was that reported by wildlife TV presenter Iolo Williams, who recalled: "One day I watched a lek of 22 males in a beautiful valley on the Berwyn in the mid 1980s. I returned in 1995 to find only two." Most worrying has been the poor survival rate of chicks. In 1998, a survey in north Wales utilising radio tags followed young grouse from hatching and revealed that few had survived by September. Starvation and predation appeared to be the main causes for the high mortality rate.

In a last attempt to prevent the extinction of the species in Wales, the RSPB together with several Welsh conservation agencies set up The Welsh Black Grouse Recovery Programme in 1999. It was centred around six main areas in the principality, at Clocaenog, Llandegla and Ruabon Moors, North Berwyn, Migneint, Llanbrynmair and Pale. So urgent was the need for the implementation of the venture, it was able to attract considerable funding from the National Assembly for Wales and the European Union. Thankfully, some measure of success has been achieved by the programme. In 1999, numbers of males had increased to 151, and one site near Ruthin produced a remarkable 32 chicks from eight broods. Further good news followed in 2000, with an encouraging 171 males recorded, and the 2002 figure seems set to top the 200 mark. It is, perhaps, a sobering thought, that the Black Grouse, a bird with the highest conservation priority and current numbers still at a level of only 200 pairs, is now a much rarer bird in Wales than that icon of Welsh ornithology, the Red Kite.

Chough (Pyrrhocorax pyrrhocorax)

Known in Wales as *Y Frân Goesgoch* – the red-legged crow – the Chough, once widespread, is now a very rare bird. A crow of great charm and character, the Chough is easily recognisable with its blue-black velvety plumage shot with purple and green reflections and distinctive down-curved, coral red beak and legs. It is, perhaps, the most aerobatic of all crows in flight and is easily identified by its fast, swooping dives and tumbles. On the continent, the bird is often referred to as 'The Jackdaw of the Alps' because of the high altitudes at which it flies. This habit has also been witnessed at Snowdonia, where birds have been seen flying above the highest point of 3,560 feet.

In Wales, as with all Chough populations, since the latter part of the nineteenth century, numbers have decreased dramatically. In 1835, Reverend E. Dodridge Knight reported that the bird was common and bred annually at Dunraven. Other reports, from the 1840s, stated that the Chough was plentiful around the Welsh coast from Tenby to Dinas, nesting regularly in the ruins of the Bishop's palace at St. David's and witnessed "in great abundance" at Manobier Castle. Yet, less than a century later, only a hundred pairs or so were to be found in the whole of the principality.

Many theories have been put forward to account for the decline in numbers. These include competition for nesting sites with jackdaws, predation of nests by egg collectors and the widespread use of gin traps. The latter, perhaps one of the most diabolical instruments of torture and death ever devised by man, certainly had a significant effect on Chough populations. Three specimens of the bird now residing in the National Museum of Wales bear witness to the carnage caused by this steel slayer of innocent creatures. All

three were found in a consignment of Pembrokeshire rabbits, having met cruel deaths in gin traps. Egg collectors, too, must have contributed to the fall in numbers, with clutches being stolen from nests on Bardsey Island, annually, up until the late 1940s. This mindless practice has continued until recent times, with one site in Snowdonia reportedly robbed year after year. Man's brutal assault on Chough populations has been comprehensive and there are even accounts of the bird being slain for the dinner table. Early last century, numbers of the birds, known as 'Billy Cocks', were on open sale at Swansea market, and were apparently much prized by visiting French seamen.

In 1982, a Chough survey of Wales estimated numbers of birds at 140 pairs. Whilst this, at first sight, appeared to be a significant improvement on the 100 pairs witnessed in a survey held in 1963, it seems likely the latter search was more exhaustive and, at best, the bird had held its own over the twenty-year period. The fact that numbers had not declined further can, perhaps, best be accounted for by the ban on gin traps and, possibly, a dramatic decline in populations of the Peregrine Falcon – a natural predator of the Chough. Current numbers are put at 180 pairs, which represents two thirds of the entire British population. The coast of Pembrokeshire, particularly Ramsey Island and the Castlemartin Peninsula, is home to almost sixty pairs; whilst in north Wales, ninety or so pairs show a preference for the artificial cliff sites of abandoned mines and quarries. One encouraging statistic is that of a pair nesting on the Gower Peninsula, after an absence of almost a hundred years.

Certainly, numbers in Wales appear to have stabilised and are even increasing slightly. However, although trapping and other predation by man has almost been eradicated, chemicals used in the treatment of livestock may still represent a threat to Chough numbers. Recent studies, too, have shown that the conservation of the species in Wales may be dependent on the continued presence of grazing animals. The birds' diet consists mainly of soil invertebrates such as beetles, ants and worms that are unearthed by the use of its strong bill. When traditional feeding sites are left ungrazed by livestock local decline in numbers has been recorded.

Greenland White-Fronted Goose (*Anser albifrons flavirostris*)

A winter visitor to Wales, the Greenland White-Fronted Goose is one of the rarest geese in the world. First discovered to be a separate race from the European species by Sir Peter Scott and C. T. Dalgety as recently as 1948, the main distinguishing characteristic of Greenland species of whitefront is its orange bill, instead of the pink bill of the European race. In addition, the larger Greenland birds are noticeably darker in colouration. Mainly grey-brown with strong dark barring on the underparts, the bird was given the name white-front by Welsh eighteenth century naturalist Thomas Pennant, in his *British Zoology* of 1776, after the broad white band at the base of the bill.

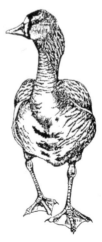

During the 1950s, the entire world population was estimated at 17,500–23,000 birds. However, by the late 1970s numbers had fallen significantly, to around 14,000–16,000. A stark illustration of the decline has been witnessed in Wales, where numbers have fallen from a high of more than 1,100 to just 100 birds. Reasons for the decline appear to be a combination of loss of peatland habitats, bad winter weather and over-shooting.

Populations were once witnessed at two main sites in Wales, at the Dyfi estuary and also at Cors Caron. At this latter site, birds traditionally started to arrive in late October and, by January each year, around 500–600 birds would gather and remain until April. However, disaster struck when the severe winter conditions of 1962/3 hit populations particularly hard. Five hundred birds arrived in 1962 but, unable to unlock the icy grip on their food plants, many starved to death. Matters were made worse by indiscriminate shooting, and there were even reports of geese so weak from hunger that they were easy prey for men with sticks. Of the estimated 500, only a third survived to depart after the spring thaw. Successive seasons saw further declines in numbers until 1968, when the site was abandoned altogether.

The first real historical account of whitefronts on the Dyfi estuary was made by H. E. Forrest in his *The Vertebrate Fauna of North Wales* of 1907, when he describes the geese as being common. By the mid 1970s, numbers of the Greenland race there had fallen to a mere 38. Undoubtedly, numbers began to recover when estuary wildfowlers imposed a voluntary ban on shooting the bird, and, by 1987, numbers had risen to 108. Welsh populations for the winter of 2000/1 were put at between 80 and 160 birds and, the following season, a count revealed around 120 individuals. Since a significant number of the world population of the species winters on the Dyfi estuary, it is clear that Wales has an international responsibility for the conservation of these birds.

Lapwing (*Vanellus vanellus*)

Once a familiar wader of farmland, moor and marsh, the Lapwing, also known by the country name 'peewit', is easily recognised in the air by its characteristic silhouette and clumsy wing beats. The name Lapwing is derived from the Old English *hleapwince*, meaning 'a leap with a waver in it', which perhaps aptly describes its nuptial display flight. It is a handsome bird with its distinctive crest, white cheek patches and black and white breast plumage. Seen from a distance, the bird's upper plumage appears black but closer

examination reveals it to be deep bottle green, hence yet another common name, that of Green Plover. Historically, Lapwings declined in the 19th century due to the drainage and enclosure of farmland and commercial egg gathering for food. Following the Lapwing Act of 1926 that limited egg gathering, numbers increased before declining again from the 1950s onwards. Over the last 30 years or so the bird has struggled to cope with changing agricultural practices, particularly the switch to autumn sown crops.

Numbers of birds in Wales are annually swelled during the winter with an influx of individuals from the rest of Britain and mainland Europe, especially during periods of harsh weather conditions. Indeed, that the bird was once so numerous in some parts of the principality during winter can be judged by a 1970 report from Gwent. It revealed that in fields around Magor, a flock of no less than 15,000 birds was witnessed. Sadly, such sights are very much a thing of the past. There were 15,000 breeding pairs in Wales during the 1970s and even as recently as 1987, numbers were put at 7,500. However, by 1998

numbers had fallen to just 1,689 – a staggering 73% decline in little over a decade. The reasons for such a dramatic decline in the fortunes are not hard to find and are inevitably linked to changes in agricultural practices. Ideal lapwing terrain is a mixture of spring-tilled fields for nesting and grassland for chicks to forage in. Sadly, the combination of these in Wales has become increasingly rare. Undoubtedly, more widespread use of pesticides and an increase in numbers of man's animals has had an adverse effect too. BTO surveys show that fields where birds nested annually have been deserted when stock move in, and at sites where birds remain, efforts at nesting are often thwarted. Iolo Williams has described the plight of the bird in Wales as "dire", and added: "The switch from cattle to sheep farming partly explains it. Grass is grazed much shorter and increasing stock densities mean more nests and chicks are trampled on…"

Having disappeared completely from large tracts of land in the principality, the Lapwing has become a species of the highest conservation concern in Wales. The future of the bird with the plaintive, haunting cry and tumbling flight would appear to be bleak, unless a regime of more environmentally sensitive farming practices and active habitat management can be maintained.

Peregrine Falcon (*Falco peregrinus*)

Known in Welsh as *Hebog Tramor*, the Peregrine Falcon, the very epitome of avian aerial strength and speed, is Wales's largest falcon. Instantly recognisable, the pale, finely barred underparts of the bird contrast with the slate-grey upper plumage, black head and distinctive moustache-like cheek stripe. When in flight, its silhouette resembles an anchor, due to its long wings and short tail. A magnificent aerobat, during a dive or 'stoop', the Peregrine is believed to attain speeds of up to 200 km an hour.

Hailed since earliest times as one of nature's surest and most magnificently skilled natural hunters, the speed, agility and power of the bird has long been harnessed by man for his own use. Certainly, falconry in one form or another has existed since 2000 BC and was widespread in Europe by 300 BC. In Wales, the 10th century laws of Hywel Dda refer to the entitlement of the king's court to nestlings and, from about 1173, King Henry II sent annually to the sea cliffs of Pembrokeshire for young peregrines. From the thirteenth century, falconry came to be regarded as the noblest of arts. So fashionable did the sport become, that the Peregrine Falcon was given the protection of the crown and harsh penalties were handed out to those who dared harm one. However, by the late eighteenth century, game shooting had become more popular and the tide

began to turn against the Peregrine. The once protected falcon became an enemy and was in its turn hunted and shot. As if such predation of the bird was not enough, by the beginning of the nineteenth century, man's assault on peregrine populations included the new craze of egg collecting. Beginning as a pastime for leisured Victorian gentlemen, the hobby soon became common amongst all classes and the peregrine egg, regarded as amongst the most beautiful laid by any bird, was eagerly sought after. That the cruel practice had an effect on peregrine numbers is beyond doubt, and it is certain that records from Wales such as the one where two collectors took 35 clutches from two Breconshire peregrine sites in the years 1912–38, was but one account of a very widespread problem.

During the Second World War the government ordered the destruction of peregrines due to the threat they posed to pigeons carrying messages of national importance. With official approval, significant numbers of nests in Wales were raided, notably in Pembrokeshire and Caernarvonshire, and eggs and chicks destroyed. Adult birds were also culled and, not surprisingly, numbers declined. After the war, populations recovered somewhat before again being hit by the widespread agricultural use of pesticides such as DDT. So catastrophic were the effects of the deadly organo-phosphates, that, during the 1960s, peregrine numbers were reduced to one or two pairs in the whole of Wales. Ironically, the plight of the bird in the principality was only fully appreciated because pigeon fanciers in the South Wales valleys began to protest loudly about the high number of birds in the principality. Thanks to the misguided protesters, the insidious threat that chemicals represented, not only to the peregrine population but all wildlife, was recognised. With a ban on the use of the most harmful toxins in place, peregrine numbers began to recover again. At the time of the last UK survey in 1991, the Welsh population was estimated to be a healthy 259 pairs.

Perhaps the biggest threat to the bird today comes from those same pigeon fanciers who were unwittingly instrumental in saving the bird. Mistakenly believing the bird has a major impact on racing pigeons, they resort to laying live poisoned baits near eyries. Recent years have seen an increase in the callous and illegal practice, mostly in south Wales. In fact, according to Government statistics, Peregrines account for only three per cent of racing pigeon deaths, most failing to return after becoming lost, exhausted or colliding with overhead electricity cables.

Puffin *(Fratercula arctica)*

Of all the birds that inhabit the coastline and offshore islands of Wales there can scarcely be one as instantly recognisable as the Puffin. A short, stocky bird around 30 cm high, the Puffin has glossy black upper parts and white undersides and face, the latter marked with a distinctive black line across the eye that gives it a characteristic

sorrowful look. The most prominent and appealing feature, however, is the triangular beak. Bright glossy red-orange at the tip and blue-grey near the base, the two equal areas of colour are divided by a pale yellow ridge. So overlarge and conspicuous is its bill, that in Wales the puffin has come to be referred to as the 'bottlenose' or 'sea parrot'. A member of the Auk family, which includes the Guillemots and Razorbills, Puffins are skilful fishers, able to catch and hold up to a dozen or so of their favourite sand eel prey in their gaudy parrot-like beaks.

Estimates have put the total world population of the Puffin at 15 million birds. Although the importance of British and Irish populations, which have been calculated as being approximately a seventh of this figure, cannot be underestimated, it would appear they have declined dramatically over the past century. In contrast to estimated numbers today, for instance, nineteenth century reports of populations on offshore Welsh islands tell of colonies so large that words could not adequately describe such huge numbers. That a thriving colony once existed on Grassholm is confirmed by a report from photographers who visited the island in 1890 and estimated there were over half a million birds nesting there. A few years later, Cardiff naturalist Robert Drane, commenting on the multitude of puffin burrows on the west Wales island, said: "You may tread upon the ground which is so hollowed by their galleries that at every step it gives way and buries them by the dozens in the falling soil." Eventually, it appears, such extensive burrowing resulted in the collapse and erosion of the soil and brought about an evacuation of the island in favour of nearby Skomer and Skokholm. To this day, these two Pembrokeshire coast islands boast the largest breeding populations in southern Britain, with numbers on Skokholm put at 5,000 and Skomer 10,000 birds. Such figures, though, show an alarming decrease when compared with those of only a half a century ago, when populations were put at 20,000 and 50,000 respectively. The reasons for such dramatic declines in numbers are not fully understood but may be due to a number of factors such as climatic change, seaborne pollution, which can affect food supply, and human disturbance.

It is believed that rats were probably responsible for the destruction of the puffin colony on Ramsey Island that was reported in the early eighteenth century as being enormous. Around this time, the bird was extensively harvested for the table by mainlanders. The flesh of the bird is dark and is said to possess a fishy flavour, which no doubt led to the curious belief that it was a 'bird fish' and thus suitable for consumption during Lent. Such confusion was commented on by George Owen in his book *Description of Penbrokshire* of 1603: "the puffine, a bird in all respectes bredd of byrdes of his kinde by layeing egges feathered and flieing with other birds in the ayre, and yet is reputed to be fishe, the reason I cannot learne."

If any Welsh island should be considered an appropriate setting for a colony of *Fratercula arctica* then surely it would be Priestholm, more commonly known as Puffin Island. In 1662, John Ray recorded seeing large numbers of the bird on the aptly named limestone isle situated off the Anglesey coast. So, too, did Thomas Pennant in 1773, who commented: "Puffins incessantly squall round, alight and disappear into their burrows; or come out, stand erect, gaze at you in a most grotesque manner, then take flight." Large numbers still colonised the island around the beginning of this century but since then populations have been in steady decline. Today, less than a hundred pairs remain. Although it is certain that a colony of puffins once existed on Cardigan Island, accurate numbers are difficult to ascertain. One report from a sheep grazier from the early part of this century described the bird as being widespread on the island. Yet the earliest reliable report, by Bertram Lloyd in 1924, put numbers at less than fifty pairs. Whatever the bird's status was, it appears rats that escaped from the storm wrecked liner *Herefordshire* in 1934 eventually accounted for all of them.

Red Kite (*Milvus milvus*)

If one single avian species were to represent the majesty of Welsh birds, then it must surely be the Red Kite. The striking beauty and masterly aerial skills of a raptor regarded by many as the national bird of Wales are, perhaps, unrivalled by any bird of prey in Europe. Its glowing, chestnut-red body plumage, pale grey head and dazzling white wing patches all add up to a bird of breathtaking beauty. To witness the Red Kite flying free in its native Wales for the first time is a not easily forgotten sight. Victorian naturalist William Warde Fowler enthusiastically recorded his first glimpse of a bird in 1869, above the Tywi valley: "The sun lit up the red colour of his back and tail, and as he turned, the rusty feathers of his underparts. The wings were narrow, with the primaries standing out distinct

from each other like a crow's; the tail long, the fork most distinct, as if a deep segment of a circle had been cut out of it."

Around the time Warde Fowler was marvelling at the graceful flight of his first Welsh kite, the species was plummeting towards extinction. Remarkably, once the most common British bird of prey, man's nineteenth century guns, traps and poisons nearly spelt the end of the bird not only in Wales but the whole of Britain. By 1870 it had been eradicated from England and, twenty years later, it had gone from Scotland. Only in the isolated sessile oak woodlands of the Tywi and Cothi valleys did a few pairs manage to survive into the twentieth century. With efforts by farmers, landowners and volunteer conservationists in monitoring and protecting the last few nests from egg robbers and skin collectors, the species pulled back from the very edge of extinction.

Throughout the first fifty years of the twentieth century, the spectre of extinction continued to hover over the species, with recorded numbers of birds remaining at less than a dozen pairs. The early 1950s saw a slight improvement in the fortunes of the bird, with around twenty recorded pairs before myxomatosis struck a savage blow by reducing the numbers of the kites' rabbit prey. The following decade, another factor in inhibiting any increase in numbers occurred, when the insidious effects of agricultural organo-chlorine compounds resulted in two thirds of all clutches of eggs failing to hatch. When use of the deadly chemicals was banned, numbers began to slowly increase. By the mid 1970s 20 pairs were recorded and in 1984 a target figure of fifty pairs was reached.

Despite such encouraging successes, the bird remained vulnerable to the misguided actions of gamekeepers and un-scrupulous egg collectors. For instance, in 1990, ten kites, which then represented five per cent of the entire British population, were found poisoned in Wales. The same year, at least half a dozen nests were robbed of precious clutches of eggs. So serious a threat did egg collectors become, that, the following year, the British Army were called in to protect the most vulnerable nests. With improved protection, numbers began to soar and in 1993 numbers reached the 100 pair milestone. Today, as a result of the longest running conservation project of its kind anywhere in the world, more than 200 pairs of Red Kites grace the skies of the principality. In 1999, the Red Kite was voted 'bird of the century' by the British Trust For Ornithology. It was an accolade richly deserved by a bird aptly described by a spokesman for the *Kite Country Project* as being: "…a symbol of the beauty and richness of rural Wales. So rare, so beautiful and so Welsh."

Roseate Tern (*Sterna dougallii*)

It is no exaggeration to state that the extremely rare and beautiful Roseate Tern is in grave danger of disappearing from the shores of Wales forever. A member of the Laridae family of birds, it can be distinguished from other species of terns by its slightly paler upper parts, longer tail streamers and shallow wing beats when in flight. In addition, perhaps its most distinctive feature is its summer plumage, a distinctive rosy-tinted breast from which the bird takes its name. It is a summer visitor, arriving on Welsh shores to breed during the end of April and departing again for warmer climes around the end of August. In Wales, a small breeding colony exists on the north of Anglesey.

The bird has had a chequered history in Wales, and whilst it could never have been described as abundant, the species can rarely have been as perilously close to extinction in the principality as it is today. In common with all species of birdlife, during the nineteenth century the Roseate Tern suffered terribly from the guns of so-called sportsmen. So drastic was the drop in numbers that it soon began disappearing from its traditional haunts at an alarming rate. By the turn of the century, its status was little better, although it continued to maintain a tenuous foothold in Wales. A report in *The Zoologist* of March 1906 stated: "The Roseate Tern is not abundant on the Skerries. It is impossible to give its numbers exactly, but at a rough estimate there cannot be more than one pair to six or seven hundred or perhaps fewer of the dominant species..." As well as the Skerries site, small colonies once existed on the islands of Grassholm and Skokholm.

Gradually numbers began to recover and by the 1950s the total British population was estimated to be a respectable 1,000 pairs. Since then, however, the species has again undergone a drastic decline. By 1969 numbers had fallen to around 650 pairs, and 1987 estimates put the entire British population at around 110 pairs. Populations in Wales fared even worse. In the mid 1980s, Welsh roseates numbered 200 pairs but within a few short years only forty pairs remained. Since then, despite a minor recovery in 1988, when 45 pairs were recorded, the trend has been dramatically downwards. The reasons for the decline in numbers is not fully understood but, certainly, natural predators have played their part; there is for instance a report of Peregrine Falcons accounting for 36 adult Welsh birds in 1980 alone. Similarly, at the same site, twelve adults fell victim to a single fox in 1987. It is, however, possible that other factors, such as a preoccupation with trapping by young boys at the birds' wintering grounds in West Africa, have also taken a heavy toll. In addition, chicks in their shallow nests on open, sandy shores have become victim to recent cold wet spring weather in Wales, which has also made it difficult for adult birds to obtain their diet of small fish and marine crustaceans.

In 1991, the then RSPB Species Officer and spokesman Iolo Williams was to report: "There are now just five pairs on Anglesey and a danger that they may be gone for good soon." Just over a decade later, such words appear prophetic. The 2000 breeding season was a disaster, with none of the three clutches of eggs laid hatching and, thus, no young Welsh birds fledging. The current population in Wales stands at a miserable three breeding pairs, which nest at Cemlyn, near Amlwch, on Anglesey. The site is designated as a Special Protection Area (SPA) as part of a UK-wide network to protect the species, with nests closely monitored by wardens from the North Wales Wildlife Trust. Clearly, the future of the bird in the principality is precarious, with the threat of extinction within the next decade a real possibility.

MAMMALS

Wales has a rich and varied mammal fauna. Indeed, 44 species have been recorded in the principality in recent times. Included are four species of deer, three varieties of shrew, four types of mice, three voles and eleven species of bats. The commonest is believed to be the ubiquitous Brown Rat (*Rattus norvegicus*); the rarest, almost certainly, Bechstein's Bat (*Myotis bechsteinii*).

Yet, as varied as the Welsh mammal fauna is today, it is missing many species that once graced the principality. For example, it appears the European Beaver (*Castor fiber*) was once a native species. Giraldus Cambrensis made reference to beavers on the River Teifi in 1188 and added that they were found nowhere else in England or Wales. The Wolf (*Canis lupus*), too, was once on the list of Welsh fauna. The last one was probably killed in the sixteenth century although, curiously, Robert Prys Morris, in his *Cantref Meirionydd*, tells of one being despatched at Ogo'r Fleiddiast, near Dolgellau, in 1785. The spectacular carnivore the Wildcat (*Felis silvestris*) was probably once native but disappeared even from wildest Wales sometime in the nineteenth century. Though never native, but introduced from Scotland in the 1880s for 'sport', the Mountain Hare (*Lepus timidus*) seems to have flourished on the isolated uplands of Wales, at least for a while. J. G. Millais, in his *The Mammals of Great Britain & Ireland* of 1905, confirmed as much: "…they are now common on the Snowdon range, forty or fifty being sometimes killed in a day's shooting." Such predation eventually took its toll and by the latter half of the twentieth century, the species was thought to have died out. However, as recently as the winter of 1969–70, four mountain hares were recorded, by

Nature Conservancy staff, on high ground in Caernarvonshire. Another mammal to have disappeared in recent times is the Black Rat (*Rattus rattus*). Accidentally introduced from the Near East during the Middle Ages, it survived in the principality, mainly in the south Wales ports of Cardiff, Newport and Swansea, until the 1970s.

Of the mammals that grace the Welsh landscape today, one creature that could go the same way as the beaver or wolf in Wales is the Water Vole (*Arvicola terrestris*). A recent catastrophic decline of 89%, largely attributed to predation by the introduced North American Mink (*Mustela vison*), means the once common and widespread mammal could be extinct in Wales by 2010 if measures are not taken. On a happier note, Wales remains the stronghold of the rare Lesser Horsehoe Bat (*Rhinolophus hipposideros*). Of the 17,000 British population, an estimated 10,000 are found in Wales. Welsh numbers of the Grey Seal (*Halichoerus grypus*), too, are considered of national and international importance. The 5,000 found around the western coastline of the principality represent two per cent of the world population. Fourteen species of cetacean have been recorded in Welsh waters in recent times. As well as being home to a colony of Bottlenose Dolphins, Cardigan Bay also has numbers of Common Dolphin (*Delphinus delphis*), Risso's Dolphin (*Grampus griseus*) and Harbour Porpoise (*Phocoena phocoena*). This latter species, which is severely threatened, is also frequently seen in the waters off Bardsey Island, Cemaes Head, Ramsey Sound, Strumble Head, Skomer Island and the Gower Peninsula.

Because of their secretive, often nocturnal habits, the status of some Welsh mammals is unknown. True numbers of three species of mice (Harvest, Dormouse and Yellow-neck) and the same number of bats (Brandt's, Barbastelle, and Bechstein), for instance, remain unclear. It is certain, however, that the latter are only occasionally recorded and are extremely rare within Wales.

Bottlenose Dolphin (*Tursiops truncatus*)

Bottlenose Dolphins range widely throughout British waters. However, the only significant colony on the whole western coast of Britain is to be found within the Special Area of Conservation (SAC) at Cardigan Bay. Members of the marine mammal order known as cetacea, the Bottlenose Dolphin is a warm-blooded, highly intelligent, air-breathing creature. Dark grey above and pale grey beneath, it normally attains a length of 2.5–4 metres and an average weight of 150–200 kg. The diet tends to be largely fish, and the Cardigan Bay dolphins' prey species include herring, mackerel, bass and mullet.

As well as the Cardigan Bay colony, solitary dolphins are often recorded around the Welsh coastline. Occasionally, individuals have behaved almost as if they were seeking human companionship. In 1975, one was regularly seen at Martin's Haven, playing with a moored dinghy and buoys; and a boatman of a passenger-carrying ferry that made daily trips to Skomer Island reported that the dolphin often accompanied him on trips and appeared to have "fallen in love" with his small brown dinghy. Named 'Bubbles' and sometimes 'Dai', it turned out that the dolphin was one and the same as the famed individual named 'Donald', who appeared to seek out human companionship at Port St. Mary 1972–74, and 'Beaky' at St. Ives and Mousehole in Cornwall in 1976.

The species is sensitive to marine pollution and during the 1980s there was an alarming increase in sightings of dead dolphins washed up on the Ceredigion coastline. At the time, there were suspicions that discharges of animal waste and the illegal dumping of industrial and agricultural chemicals were the cause. Things came to a head in 1988 with the discovery of a 10-month-old baby bottlenose at Cei Bach, north of New Quay. Analysis revealed extremely high levels of pollutants such as PCBs and DDT in its body tissue. Taking into account the fact that the young dolphin must, at the time of death, have still been suckling from its mother, conclusions were drawn that similar high levels of pollutants almost certainly existed in the adult members of

the colony. In May 1989, the Greenpeace environmental group vessel *Moby Dick* sailed into Welsh waters, to highlight the plight of the dolphins of Cardigan Bay and campaign for the establishment of Cardigan Bay as a National Marine Nature Reserve.

Today, estimates put the Cardigan Bay population at 127 with most sightings of the creature occurring along the coastline between New Quay and Cemaes Bay. Sightings in 1990 numbered 371 and 170 in 1997. The largest gathering of the species in 2001 was at Fishguard Bay, where fifty dolphins were seen, probably chasing a large shoal of fish. It is hoped a joint survey undertaken by Greenpeace and the Whale & Dolphin Conservation Society in 2002 may reveal more information about the status of the important west Wales colony.

Goat (*Capra hircus*)

High on the crags and ledges of highest Wales, eeking out a precarious living grazing sparse mountain vegetation, are flocks or 'hefts' of feral goats. Descendants of these hardy creatures appear to have existed in Wales since early times and it is likely that they were brought from the Mediterranean area of mainland Europe by Neolithic peoples around 4,000 years ago. In appearance, the feral goat is variable in colour from white with dark patches to completely grey, black or brown. The most striking features of the

animal are the horns. In the male these are large and curved, often with a spiral twist, whilst in the female they tend to be thinner and more upright. Females usually kid in late February or early March and at birth the young generally bear the same variable markings as the adults. Welsh hefts are generally confined to the mountains of Yr Eifl, Carneddau, Glyder and Snowdon, in Caernarvonshire, and Craig Aderyn, Moelwyn, Rhinog, Arennig, Rhobell Fawr and Cader Idris, in Merionethshire. A small herd also survives on the Great Orme at Llandudno that are descendants of Kashmirs imported from Windsor Great Park at the turn of the century.

One of the earliest authentic records of the remnants of the medieval herds in Snowdonia was made by Giraldus Cambrensis in 1188, when he reported that: "the wooded hills are full of goats and swine". Further mention was made in 1460 when Syr Dafydd Trefor of Anglesey wrote asking for some to be sent to him so that he could obtain their milk for medicinal purposes. His request, however, was countered by a neighbour, Gruffydd ab Tudur ab Howell, who objected to the introduction on the grounds of the damage they would cause to Anglesey's agriculture and forestry.

Thomas Pennant, the eighteenth century travelling naturalist, in his *Tours of Wales*, recorded seeing goats and noted that Welsh farmers hunted them every autumn to obtain fat for their candles, believing that tallow of goat made better candles than that of sheep or ox. He also reported that: "… the haunches of the goat are frequently salted and dried, and supply all the uses of bacon: this by the natives is called '*coch yr wden*' or hung venison…"

Man's attitude to wild goat populations has on the whole been fairly tolerant. Hill farmers, generally, readily accept the existence of feral populations, especially because of their habit of grazing cliff ledges where sheep would otherwise stray. Recent years have seen an escalation in numbers, possibly due to the recent mild winters. The once exciting glimpse of a wild goat has now become almost commonplace in some areas, with sightings even having been reported in gardens at Beddgelert. Unfortunately, with the increase in numbers has come destruction by grazing of both commercial plantations and native woodland. There have been calls for controls on numbers to be made, with claims being made that any culling would, in the long run, be in the interest of the species as a whole. In 2002, forty of the two-hundred-strong Great Orme herd were relocated at two new sites in Wales and England. This followed a programme from the previous year of implanting progesterone in animals to restrict the fertility of the herd.

Greater Horseshoe Bat (*Rhinolophus ferrumequinum*)

The Greater Horseshoe Bat was once widespread throughout southern Britain, from London to Aberystwyth, with a British population of around 300,000. Sadly, today its range is now limited to south-west England and south Wales, and the entire British population is put at no more than 4–6,000 individuals. There are an estimated fourteen breeding colonies in existence, of which just three are found in Wales. A largish bat, the greater horseshoe is buff-brown in colour, weighs 10–35 g and has a wingspan of 35–40 cm. The species is easily identified at close quarters by the pronounced horseshoe-shaped skin growth on the muzzle, or, on the wing, by its heavy, butterfly-like flight with irregular stages of gliding. Its diet consists mainly of large insects such as cockchafers, noctid moths and crane flies.

The species has declined by over 90% in the last century and in Wales is only found at three nursery roosts, two in Pembrokeshire and one in Gwent. The main cause of the decline in numbers has been a reduction in insect prey due to agricultural chemical pollution and unsympathetic land management. Remedial timber treatment in roofs housing roosting sites has also had an impact by either disturbing or poisoning bats. During the late 1970s and the early 1980s, an autecological study was undertaken on a colony of greater horseshoes in Pembrokeshire. Experiments included radio tracking by use of small transmitters attached to 27 bats. Through the work, invaluable information on flight patterns, foraging behaviour and roost sites was obtained. Numbers of bats in the study colony was put at 350 individuals. This equated to a dramatic decline when compared to the 1950s, when several thousand had been recorded. Today, Pembrokeshire is the stronghold of the species in Wales, providing as it does not only two breeding sites but also important winter hibernacula in the sea caves on the Castlemartin range.

Otter (*Lutra lutra*)

A long, slender-bodied mammal with short legs and a long tapering tail, the Otter is an elusive and mostly nocturnal creature. Often its presence is only recognised by its distinctive tracks, or black, tarry droppings, or 'spraints'. Both sexes have a brown coat with a lighter throat patch, but the adult male tends to be bigger, measuring around 1.2 m and weighing 10 kg, some 25% larger than the female. Its diet is mainly fish, especially eels, but it will take amphibians and, occasionally, small birds or mammals.

Historically, the Otter was in former times widespread throughout Wales and common enough to be hunted by organised otter hunts. However, during the period 1950–1970, populations throughout the principality crashed, due mainly to pollution of its habitat from persistent organo-chlorine agricultural pesticides. Being a carnivore, the Otter was at the top of the natural food chain. When it consumed its pollution-tainted prey, the deadly chemicals present were retained in the fatty tissue of the animal and, over a period of time, built up to deadly levels. Another cause of the decline was serious habitat loss through intensive river management. By the 1970s Welsh otter numbers had crashed. Indeed, a survey undertaken between 1977–79 revealed that the creature was only present at 20% of its former haunts in the principality, and, in some areas, for example Anglesey, it had become extinct.

In the last decade, with improvements in water quality, the Otter has made something of a comeback. Areas from which they disappeared twenty years ago have been successfully recolonised. By 1995, for instance, the species had returned to Anglesey and, in 2000, a pleasure boat captain saw a dog Otter swimming across the Menai Strait, no doubt, to further boost the population of the island. Today, the recovery continues

but is being hindered by a quite different threat, that of the motor car. Around fifty Otters are killed on the roads of Wales each year. Because of slow reproduction rates of the creature this figure represents a serious setback in the restoration of numbers in the principality. Research is currently under way to identify black spot areas and to provide solutions to reduce such mortalities.

Pine Marten (*Martes martes*)

A most graceful and strikingly beautiful animal, the extremely rare Pine Marten has been referred to as 'Snowdonia's most distinguished mammal'. Although never common, it was once resident in large areas of the principality. Sadly, its status today can, at best, be described as precarious. A member of the Mustelidae family that also includes the Weasel, Stoat and Polecat, the Pine Marten sports a coat of rich brown with an irregular yellowish or creamy-white breast patch, or 'bib', and a long bushy tail. Male adult martens, which are 53 cm in length and 1.5–2 kg in weight, tend to be larger than the typical female which measures 45 cm and weighs 1–1.5 kg. The creatures' diet consists of rodents, especially voles, frogs, insects, earthworms, berries and nuts. Although it

mainly hunts on the ground, the Pine Marten is a very adept tree climber and is quite at home in the canopy. For this reason it is known in Welsh as *Bele'r Coed* or 'cat of the tree'.

To man's shame, the Pine Marten has always been persecuted, as vermin, for its fur, or simply for 'sport'. Certainly, marten fur has always been highly prized, with capes lined with it generally only being worn by kings and princes. The AD 940 laws of the great Welsh prince Hywel Dda mention marten pelts as being worth 24 pence, quite a considerable sum and three times as much as the price paid for the pelts of the fox or otter. From early times, 'hunting the mart' became a common pastime. A twelfth century report from the Norman-Welsh squire Giraldus Cambrensis said: "Martins are very plentiful in the woods; in hunting which the day is prolonged through night by means of fires. For night coming on, a fire is lighted under the tree in which the hunted animal has taken refuge from the dogs, and being kept burning all night, the martin eyeing its brightness from the boughs above, without quitting its post, either is so fascinated by it, or, rather so much afraid of it that when morning comes the hunters find him in the same spot." Similarly, William Rowlands, a colleague of Welsh botanist Edward Lhwyd, mentions the creature in his seventeenth century notes on the wildlife of Snowdonia thus: "The Pine Martens we hunt in the same way as foxes; but a dog that chases one or two of these to death, changes his attack to no other wild beast after this, if common belief can be accepted. These animals they sometimes catch in iron traps or in a kind of basket built with stones, tempted by the entrails of raven or magpie."

Such pressures on marten populations coupled with increasing gamekeeping interests saw the extinction of the animal in south-east England and southern Wales by the 1880s. This was quickly followed by the disappearance of the animal from north-east England and south Scotland by about 1900. In the wildest parts of Wales it clung on, but a survey from 1994 suggested the creature was "functionally extinct" in the principality. However, a Vincent Wildlife Trust database of marten sightings since 1990 reveals more than 300 encounters, mostly in Caernarvonshire, Carmarthenshire and Merionethshire. Certainly, the Pine Marten does still exist in Wales, but its current status and future prospects remain uncertain.

Polecat (*Mustela putorius*)

Described as: "The mammalogists' spiritual equivalent of the quintessentially Welsh Red Kite", the Polecat was once confined in Britain to the wilder parts of Wales. A member of the Mustalidae family, the Polecat is often referred to as the 'foumart' because of its habit of emitting a foul stench when alarmed. Larger than the Stoat and Weasel but smaller than the Otter, the adult male Polecat normally measures 45–60 cm and weighs 7–18 kg. Female Polecats are considerably smaller than the male. The usual colouration is one of a darkish brown; however, this outer coat is coarse and rather sparse so that the creamy coloured underfur shows through in places. The face, with its 'masked bandit' look, is marked with patches of white around the mouth, behind the eyes and along the edges of the small rounded ears. There have also been sightings of individuals in Wales sporting a reddish coat. The first of these erythristic forms were shot at Cors Caron around 1903 and promptly sent to an Aberystwyth taxidermist. Since then, however,

such animals have only been witnessed infrequently and appear to be restricted to the isolated areas of north Ceredigion and south Merionethshire. The creatures' diet consists of rabbits, rats, fish and other small mammals and birds. Frogs are also freely taken and, in Wales, it was once widely believed that, each spring, polecats migrated in large numbers to the peat bog of Tregaron, to take advantage of the large numbers of spawning frogs. However, there seems to be little conclusive proof of this.

Known in Welsh as the *Ffwlbart*, the creature was, up until the time of the First World War, both widespread and abundant throughout Britain. However, such was the extent of trapping by gamekeepers, early in the century, the species had been wiped out in both England and Scotland. In Wales, too, the creature was subjected to merciless persecution, with one report alone claiming more than five hundred being accounted for in the years 1926–31. In the wilder parts of the principality, however, where there were few gamekeepers and little game, the polecat continued to flourish. From this small population, the species has spread to most parts of Wales and has even made inroads over the border into England again.

Today, the greatest threat to the species in Wales appears to be the motor car. In recent times, road casualties have become commonplace. One theory about why the creature has not established itself fully in the valleys of south Wales suggests that it is because of the high mortality on urban roads. Despite this, populations in the principality remain reasonably healthy. A Vincent Wildlife Trust survey of 1999 estimated the Polecat population of Wales to be 16,700.

Red Squirrel (*Sciurus vulgaris*)

The Red Squirrel was once widespread throughout Wales but in the last century has undergone a dramatic decline. One of the main reasons for the fall in numbers has been the introduction of the North American Grey Squirrel (*Sciurus carolinensis*). The first official record of greys being released into the wild is at Henbury Park, Cheshire, in

1876. However, it appears that the species had, in fact, been resident in Wales at a much earlier date. In the *Cambrian Quarterly* of 1830 it was revealed: "…in some retired glades of Mongomeryshire and Denbighshire a Grey Squirrel is found. Between Llanfair Caer Einon and Llan Eurvyl… is a deep woody dingle called Cwm Llwynog… here a Grey Squirrel lives and breeds… I have also seen a very fine stuffed specimen of the Welsh Grey Squirrel in the possession of a gentleman residing in Chester; it was shot near Llandisilio Hall, Denbighshire in October 1828."

Despite its relative rarity, few people would be unfamiliar with the picture-book image of the Red Squirrel. Reddish-brown with greyish-white underparts and long bushy tail and ornamental ear tufts, it measures 30–50 cm and weighs 250–350 g. Its diet consists of seeds, berries, acorns and, occasionally, eggs and young birds. The arrival of the greys nearly spelt the end for the reds in Wales. Research has revealed that, once the introduced squirrels arrive in an area, within fifteen years the Red Squirrels will be displaced. Competition for food, a lower birth rate and a greater susceptibility to a Parapox virus appear to be the main factors in the reds losing out to the greys. Almost overnight, it seemed, the Red Squirrel disappeared from large parts of the principality. Today, there are estimated to be only around 1,000 left in Wales. The largest single colony is at the Clocaenog Forest, near Ruthin, in Denbighshire, but numbers are also found in the Tywi, Crychan and Irfon woodlands, in Carmarthenshire, and on Anglesey. This latter colony at Pentraeth, has, with the help of the *Anglesey Red Squirrel Project* and the removal of 4,500 greys, recently shown an encouraging increase in numbers, from 40 in 1998 to around a hundred in 2000. There are also plans to start a new colony at Newborough Forest, possibly with individuals taken from captive stock.

Skomer Vole (*Clethrionomys glareolus skomerensis*)

Lying off the Marloes Peninsula on the Pembrokeshire coast of Wales is the unique island National Nature Reserve of Skomer. Besides being a priceless sea-bird sanctuary, in season, the island displays a breathtaking floral display and is home to a number of mammal species. Perhaps the most famous denizen of this island retreat is a unique sub-species of bank vole – the celebrated Skomer Vole. First claimed as a unique species by Cardiff chemist Robert Drane in 1897, the vole is somewhat larger, on average 10 g heavier, and the upper parts are more bright reddish than the mainland variety. One of its most remarkable and endearing qualities is its tameness. This is best illustrated by its toleration of handling by man, without protest. One observer noted this and remarked of the species that it: "Will sit quietly in the hand and eat a proferred crumb."

Drane began visiting the islands off Pembrokeshire in the early 1890s. On one such visit in June 1896, he wrote: "Caught a little animal which I do not recognise as of any British species that I know. It is larger and more highly coloured than the bank vole. I have never seen a Bank Vole like this one." On 4 January 1897, he addressed a meeting of the Cardiff Naturalists' Society and pointed out the differences in size, colouration and teeth and referred to the species as: "my skomer vole". The mystery regarding the origins of the vole has long puzzled scientists. One school of thought was that it was descended from an earlier immigrant race that was once widespread on the mainland and reached the island when sea levels were significantly lower. When a smaller race arrived later and ousted the larger species on the mainland, sea levels had risen sufficiently to prevent it from reaching Skomer. Thus, there the larger vole continued to flourish. Generally, however, scientists gave little credence to such a theory, believing rather that the vole was derived from the mainland species, possibly brought over to Skomer by settlers who built iron age enclosures there about 2000 years ago. Such a belief is widely held today, for it is now generally accepted that island species under conditions of isolation tend to develop certain characteristics that differ from the original mainland variety. There are, for instance, similar examples of variation to be found in sub species of field vole found in Guernsey and the Orkney Islands. Today, the Skomer Vole, which has a population of around 21,000, has been relegated to the status of a sub-species. To many, however, such a demotion in classification in no way detracts from the uniqueness of the tiny mammal that is literally Skomer's own vole.

AMPHIBIANS & REPTILES

A long with the invertebrates, amphibians and reptiles have, in the last fifty years, suffered more than any other category of wildlife in Wales. Inevitably, their vulnerability and restriction in range has been linked to their specific habitat requirements. Amphibian populations have been affected by wholesale changes in land management and agricultural practices, with drainage and pollution being the major factors in the decline in numbers. Six amphibian species are native to Wales: one frog, the Common Frog (*Rana temporaria*); two species of toad, the Common (*Bufo bufo*) and Natterjack (*Bufo calamita*); and three species of newt, the Palmate (*Triturus helveticus*), Smooth (*Triturus vulgaris*) and Great Crested (*Tritus cristatus*). Of the half dozen species, two are particularly under threat. The Great Crested Newt, whilst not exactly rare, has undergone significant population decline and is considered at risk. Two of the largest colonies in Britain are found at Johnstown, near Wrexham, and Deeside and Buckley in north-east Flintshire. A warning of what could befall the Greated Crested Newt is the example of the Natterjack Toad, that became extinct in Wales in the 1960s.

Loss or degradation of habitat on which they depend has also affected reptiles. There are five land reptile species found in the principality, three lizards, Common Lizard (*Lacerta vivipara*), Sand Lizard, Slow Worm (*Anguis fragilis*) and two snakes, the Adder (*Vipera berus*) and Grass Snake (*Natrix natrix*). The Green Lizard (*Lacerta viridis*) was introduced into Wales in 1931, at Portmeirion, but the small population, presumably unable to adapt to the Welsh climate, disappeared shortly afterwards. The same fate befell the native Sand Lizard, which became extinct in Wales 40 years ago. Like the amphibians, reptiles are extremely vulnerable to changes in land usage and are also slow colonisers. Taking these factors into account, and that they have to spend half the year undisturbed in hibernation, it is, perhaps, hardly surprising they have declined in numbers and range.

Three species of marine turtle have been recorded around the coastline of Wales. Sightings of live creatures and records of individuals washed up on Welsh shores have been relatively common. Four sightings for 1990 alone were recorded of the Loggerhead Turtle (*Caretta Caretta*) and as recently as 1999 one was seen off the Gower Coast.

The largest-ever recorded Leatherback Turtle (*Dermochelys coriacea*), which measured 2.91 metres and weighed 916 kg, was beached at Morfa Harlech in 1988. And in 1999, a rare Kemp's Ridley Turtle (*Lepidochelys kempii*) was found alive at Broadhaven, in Pembrokeshire. Because of its rarity – only a few thousand are believed to exist – the female turtle was flown to Florida to join a captive breeding programme.

Natterjack Toad (*Bufo calamita*)

One of two species of toad recorded in Wales, the Natterjack Toad is found at around sixty sites in Britain. Like the Sand Lizard, its presence in the principality today is due to a reintroduction programme since native Natterjacks disappeared from Wales forty years ago.

Smaller than the Common Toad (*Bufo bufo*), the Natterjack Toad attains a length of 6–8 cm. Main characteristics that distinguish the species from the common kind are a yellow stripe down the centre of its back, the fact that it runs rather than hops and its harsh, penetrating call. Secretive and generally nocturnal, the habitat requirements for the species are light, sandy soils, into which individuals can dig themselves during daytime, and shallow pools to spawn. The breeding season extends from early spring through to July, when spawn, as in the case of the Common Toad, is laid in strings.

Under pressure from housing and tourist development, the species became extinct in the principality when the last colony disappeared from the north Wales coast in the 1960s. However, at the turn of the century, a plan to reintroduce the toad got under way. At a specialised sandy habitat, shallow pools were created and spawn was transported from Merseyside, where Natterjack numbers are healthy. To the delight of the scientists involved in the project, in 2001, 96 of Britain's rarest amphibians were recorded at the Talacre Warren, Flintshire, reintroduction site. A further transfer of Natterjack spawn was made in 2000, to a second Welsh site, this time in Denbighshire. And whilst it is too early to judge results yet, hopes are high that the Talacre reintroduction success will be repeated.

Sand Lizard (*Lacerta agilis*)

The Sand Lizard is the rarest of the three species of lizard found in Britain. Populations have seriously declined throughout Britain and indeed disappeared completely from its former haunts on the dunes of west and north Wales. Only a coordinated effort at captive breeding and reintroduction has seen the species again grace the principality. A stocky, short-legged reptile, the Sand Lizard measures 15–20 cm long. It is active during April–October and hibernates in underground burrows for the remainder of the year. The males are greyish-green in colour and the females brown. Both sexes have dark spots with whitish centres on their backs and sides. During the breeding season of May–June, the flanks of the male turn a distinctive vivid green. Females lay 3–15 eggs in sandy sites exposed to the sun. The exacting habitat requirements of the species and inappropriate land management saw it become extinct in Wales in the 1960s. Its former stronghold in the principality was duneland from Prestatyn to the Point of Air. However, increasing building in the area, especially for tourist development, spelt the end for the species in Wales. William Condry, in his *The Natural History of Wales* of 1981, was to note with some regret: "If conservation had come on the scene half a century earlier than it did it might have saved those lizards. Instead the shacks got there first."

In the early 1990s, a captive breeding programme was undertaken in an effort to restore the species to Wales. Adult Sand Lizards were captured at Ainsdale National Nature Reserve on the Sefton Coast, north of Liverpool, and transferred to an open air vivarium at Chester Zoo. Within twelve months they were breeding and, in 1995, juvenile Sand Lizards were released on a national nature reserve in north-west Wales. The reserve site was chosen not only for the thick vegetation and open sandy areas but also because of a lack of predators such as domestic cats. Further releases were made in successive years and, in 1998, the first Welsh breeding record for the species in four decades was confirmed with the sighting of three hatchlings. Proof of the continuing success of the programme came the following year, when four more newly hatched young were recorded.

FISH

Wales has some of the finest rivers in Britain. The Wye, Usk, Tywi and Teifi in particular are considered of considerable ecological note; indeed, they have been recognised as being of European importance and designated as candidate Special Areas of Conservation (cSAC). The principality is also well blessed with lakes, over 400 of them. One of the finest, Llyn Tegid, the largest natural lake in Wales, has been identified as having a considerable diverse fish community, with sixteen species in all finding a home there. Biodiversity is also a characteristic of Welsh estuaries. Records for the Severn Estuary, for example, show more than a hundred kinds of fish, including seven rare migratory species.

Around forty freshwater species have been recorded in the waters of Wales, including the Welsh specialities, the Arctic Charr or *Torgoch* and Ice-age whitefish, the *Gwyniad*. Introduced species include the American Brook Trout (*Salvelnius fontinalis*) and the curious Bitterling (*Rhodeus sericeus*). Evidence of the Common Sturgeon (*Acipenser sturio*), which was once regularly recorded in Wales, particularly in the Severn, has recently become difficult to come by. Most recent records have been a 169 lb specimen, caught off the shores of Newport in Gwent in the 1980s, and a sighting of the rare vagrant fish on the Tywi in 1993. Three species of Lampreys that are considered vulnerable and are subject to international conservation legislation are found in waters of the principality. The Usk and the Wye hold good populations of the Sea Lamprey (*Petromyzon marinus*), Brook Lamprey (*Lampetra planeri*) and River Lamprey (*Lampatera fluviatilis*). Localised populations are also found on the Teifi, Tywi and Cleddau. All these sites are also important habitat for another 'at risk' fish species, the Bullhead (*Cottus gobio*).

Allis Shad (*Alosa fallax*)

Also known as the 'ale wife' and 'king of the herring', the Allis Shad is a deep-bodied fish, with a deep bluish-green back, silvery sides and white belly. Characteristically, it sports a dark blotch behind the gill covers. It is the larger of the two British shads, generally attaining a length of around 45 cm. The British shore rod-caught record is for a 2.166 kg fish but it is believed some specimens can attain a weight of 3.6 kg. Its diet consists of water fleas, shrimps and

other small crustaceans but it is likely that they do not feed when migrating. Like its relative the Twaite Shad, the Allis Shad is related to the Herring, Pilchard and Sprat and is anadromous, that is, it spends its life at sea, except for migrations into freshwater to spawn. In the past, large shoals of Severn Allis Shad have been recorded swimming inland, often as far north as Welshpool, in search of suitable spawning grounds.

Water pollution, to which shads are particularly sensitive, represents a major threat. An expert from the Countryside Council for Wales has underlined the dangers to shads in general and the Allis Shad in particular, by commenting: "It is most threatened by pollution and so it is safe to say that if you have Allis Shad in your river, you have a relatively clean river. Alas, the rivers Severn and the lower reaches of the Wye increasingly do not come into this category." Although individuals have been reported from the rivers Dee, Loughor, Severn, Tywi, Wye and Usk, it is becoming an increasingly rare fish and the existence of spawning populations, anywhere in Wales, remains doubtful. Such is the plight of the Allis Shad, that it is considered amongst the ten rarest species of fish in Britain and is included in the protected species of the Wildlife and Countryside Act 1981. Currently, conservationists are keeping their fingers crossed, hoping that numbers have been under-recorded and that the species has not disappeared entirely from the coastal waters of Wales. Such cherished hopes may not be misplaced for in 1999 the fish turned up in the River Tamar, in England, after not being recorded there for more than 120 years.

Gwyniad (*Coregonus clupeoides pennantii*)

Nestling in a fold between the Aran and Arrenig mountains, some 500 feet above sea level, the deep cold waters of Llyn Tegid are home to a unique and mysterious species of ice age fish. Often referred to as a freshwater herring or whiting (the Welsh name *Gwyniad* meaning literally whiting), the *Gwyniad* is, in fact, a true salmonoid. A silvery fish, it generally attains a size of around 30 cm and a weight of a quarter of a pound, although specimens of two pounds have been recorded. A curious characteristic of the fish is that its flesh is said by some to bear a faint smell that can be best likened to that of a cucumber. It generally feeds on tiny freshwater crustaceans and is, in turn, preyed upon by Pike that inhabit the lake. Often shoals of *Gwyniad* are witnessed leaping out of the water to escape the hungry jaws of the predatory fish. There are seven other species of freshwater whitefish to be found in British waters, including the Schelly, Pollan and Vendace, and some zoologists maintain these localised races are really all one species. According to Tate Regan, in his *Freshwater Fishes of the British Isles* of 1911, the *Gwyniad* can best be distinguished from the Schelly *(Coregoneus clupeoides stigmaticus)*, which it closely resembles, by a larger eye and a longitudinal series of scales, which consists of nine or ten in number, as opposed to seven or eight in the schelly. Despite arguments against it being unique, the *Gwyniad* has been classified as a separate sub-species, *Coregonus clupeoides pennantii.*

Although there exists a British Rod-Caught Fish Committee record for the species (1lb 7oz specimen caught by J. Williams in 1965 at Bala) the *Gwyniad* has long been known as a fish of little sporting value. A report of almost a century ago underlined this aspect of the elusive whitefish: "With respect to the *Gwyniad* I am free to confess I never yet saw one. I have been on many occasions to Bala, but I never heard of anybody taking a *Gwyniad* with a fly or bait of any kind, nor do I believe that any lure will capture these fish." Despite this, since early times, the *Gwyniad* has been caught for the table; indeed Owain Glyn-dŵr is reputed to have kept a stew pond stocked with the fish at Sycharth. It was also once a familiar item on the menus of Bala hotels; its firm, white, flesh regarded as something of a delicacy. Lord George Lyttleton of Hagley, Worcestershire, wrote in a letter of 1756: "The lake produces very fine trout and a fish called a whiting peculiar to itself and of so delicate a taste that I believe you would prefer the flavour of it to the lips of the fair maids of Bala." Similarly, Reverend Richard Warner, the well-travelled Bath historian, reported having sampled the delights of a supper of "*Gwyniads* from Bala pool" at the Bull Inn in 1798. However, Thomas Pennant, having done likewise, described the *Gwyniad* as: "a fish of insipid taste."

So secretive by nature is the *Gwyniad* and at one time so few were the recorded sightings, that it was feared that it was on the edge of extinction. Fortunately, such fears proved groundless. However, in an effort to safeguard its future, the Environmental Agency has a future plan to introduce the species to another Welsh lake with the same topography as that of Llyn Tegid.

Torgoch (*Salvelinus alpinus*)

Similar in shape to the trout, the *Torgoch* is, in fact, a member of the Salvelinus family of fish. Believed to be a landlocked ice age relative of a migratory race, it inhabits the Welsh deep-water lakes of Bodlyn, Cwellyn and Padarn. It was formerly found at Llyn Peris but was translocated to Ffynnon Llugwy in the late 1970s.

A handsome fish, the *Torgoch* has been described by E. Donovan, in his *A Natural History of British Fishes* of 1802, as: "Of an elegant, slender shape, the head long and rather pointed and its colour splendid beyond all example among indigenous fishes of this country." The upper parts of the male are greenish or bluish with a profusion of light coloured spots. For most of the year the colour-ation of the belly tends to be a very pale orange or pink. However, in the breeding season, the pale underparts are transformed into a fiery red, hence its alternative name, the 'red bellied charr of Wales'. It is thought that the predominence of red in the colouring of the fish during the spawning season led to it being named charr, after the celtic word '*cear*' meaning blood. By contrast, the female fish is a duller greenish or bluish colour.

One of the earliest references to the *Torgoch* comes from Ray, in his *Third Itinerary*, where, under the date of 26 May, 1662, he records: "They tell some fabulous stories of these fish, as that three sons of the church brought them from Rome and put them in three lakes, to wit Llanberis, Llyn Umber and Travennin into each two." Mention of the species was also made by Edward Lhwyd, who in 1684, noted: "A char is the name of a fish of the trout-kind found in Windermere in Westmorland and in a lake in Carnarvonshire by the back of Snowdon call'd Lhyn Llan Berry's." Thomas Evans, vicar of Llanberis and friend of Lhwyd, also made reference to the fish, in his letter to the botanist dated 12 August, 1693: "As for the difference of the *torgochaid*, they are of two distinct sort, those which they call he have red bellies and the she white bellies, and are never taken with any food, but by nets in the night time by Pont Fawr and in the river which is hard by the castle; they begin to catch them about the 11th. of November for a month." Certainly this description of the habits of the fish matches our present day knowledge. Spawning, which is triggered by decreasing daylight and falling water temperatures, generally occurs in November, or early December, when fish emerge en masse from the depths into the shallows. It is also at this time that the undersurface of the male changes hue, passing through shades of orange to brilliant red, from the throat to the pelvic fins, where the colouring is most intense.

During the 1970s one *Torgoch* colony came under threat when a plan for the Dinorwic pumped, storage, hydro-electric scheme was unveiled. The site chosen was at Llanberis, and the idea was to use two lakes, Llyn Marchlyn Mawr and the lower Llyn Peris as a means of obtaining kinetic energy. It was, however, considered necessary to drain Llyn Peris, to stabilise the banks and consolidate the lake bottom, to enable it to take the great surges of water that would occur once the project was complete. It was evident that conditions such as water level and temperature would afterwards prove unsuitable to the Llanberis charr. Much research, therefore, was undertaken to find a lake with similar conditions to those at Llyn Peris. The nearest suitable location proved to be Ffynnon Llugwy, another cold water glacial lake, on the slopes of the Penywaun-Wen mountains. Throughout 1978, as the waters of Llyn Peris were reduced, nets were used to trap alive the resident *Torgoch* population, who were transferred by road tanker to their new home.

Twaite Shad (*Alosa alosa*)

Smaller than *Alosa fallax*, the Twaite Shad usually attains a length of 35 cm. It is similar in colouration to the Allis Shad, except the belly tends to be yellowish-silver and it has 4 to 8 black spots behind the gill covers. Like its close relative, the Twaite Shad has come to be known by a variety of names such as the 'goureen', 'chad' and 'queen of the herring'. In Wales, spawning populations are believed to exist in five rivers, the Loughor, Severn, Wye, Usk and Tywi. The latter, particularly, is known as a shad stronghold.

Around May time, the mature, estuarine Twaite Shad congregate in shoals in river estuaries, to prepare for their journey up-river to breed. Generally, they do not travel as far upstream as the Allis Shad but have been recorded as spawning in the Wye at Builth, after a journey of 190 km. The journey up Welsh rivers can be perilous, especially the one from the Severn. Passing through Britain's longest river, they make their way into the Wye. Here they are often taken by Stopping Boats. As they move further upstream, they are often caught at Monmouth by anglers using a bait of silver paper. From there they can fall prey to cleach net fishermen at Symonds Yat Rapids. If they reach their destination, spawning takes place at night, when 75,000–200,000 eggs are laid. Within days the ova hatch and the fry undergo rapid growth so that within two months they have attained a length of an inch. By early winter they are around four inches long, and within two years, having attained a length of around 18cm, they make their way to the sea. Adults mature after 3–4 years, when they migrate back to the parent river.

In former times, shads were a valuable food source and commercial 'shadding' for both species was undertaken utilising funnel-shaped putches. This was particularly the case on the River Severn, where the fish were extensively sold in the mining villages of the Forest of Dean and accounted for up to a third of the fishery income. Although the flesh of the Allis Shad is considered to be of superior flavour to that of its near relative, opinions vary as to either species being really suitable for the table. One report, for instance, describes the shad as: "a plebian fish excluded from all reputable banquets." Such a reputation was probably earned due to the fact that consumption of the flesh is marred by the liberal small bones, hence one of its alternative common names, the 'bony horseman'. Today, the fish are occasionally on sale at Monmouth and Gloucester markets but are mainly bought for their roes, both hard and soft, which are regarded as something of a delicacy.

As with the Allis Shad, water pollution has had a disastrous effect on British populations. Added to this, obstruction of the passage of adult fish to their traditional freshwater spawning grounds has undoubtedly had an adverse effect. In England, for instance, the species was once common in the River Thames but the construction of navigational weirs saw its extinction there. A similar fate also befell the fish at Tewkesbury, Gloucestershire. In Wales during the 1990s, there was alarm amongst conservationists at the prospect of a further decline in numbers with the proposal for the ultimately ill-fated Usk Barrage at Newport.

MOTHS & BUTTERFLIES

Of the estimated 2,600 species of moth that have been recorded within the British Isles, around 1,400 find suitable habitat amongst the diversity of the Welsh landscape, and, in the Rosy Marsh Moth, Ashworth's Rustic, the Silurian and Weaver's Wave, Wales has four species of lepidoptera found nowhere else in Britain. Other Welsh specialities include the Scarce Hooktip (*Sabra harpagula*), found in the Wye Valley, and a sub species of the Sand Hill Rustic (*Luperina nickerlii gueneei*), recorded from north Wales. Several species in the principality are under threat of extinction; these include the Transparent Burnet (*Zygaena purpuralis*), Silky Wave (*Idaea dilutaria*), Belted Beauty (*Lycia zonari britannica*), Northern Footman (*Eilema sericea*), White-spotted Pinion (*Cosmia diffinis*), and Orange Upperwing (*Jodia croceago*). As with butterflies, many moth species are dependent on a single type of habitat or food plant. Take for instance the Netted Carpet Moth (*Eustroma reticulata*), an extreme rarity found at only two locations in north Wales. The species is totally dependent on the flowers, leaves and seeds of the Yellow Balsam (*Impatiens noli-tangere*). This inevitably makes the moth extremely vulnerable to the possibility of joining the ranks of species lost and gone forever. Only active habitat management and conservation will maintain its future in the principality.

Similar efforts will have to be made on behalf of several species of butterflies. In the last hundred years, of the 59 resident British species, fifteen have declined and five have become extinct. A similar picture of decline has also emerged from Wales, where the

Black-veined White (*Aporia crataegi*), Large Tortoiseshell (*Nymphalis polychloros*), Purple Emperor (*Apatura iris*), Duke of Burgundy Fritillary (*Hamearis lucina*) and the Mazarine Blue (*Cyraniris semiargus*) have all been lost in the last century. Today, undoubtedly the species in the gravest danger of disappearing from the principality is the High Brown Fritillary, which only survives in five small colonies. Not far behind is the Large Heath (*Coenonympha tullia*), of which only ten colonies remain. In 1999, Dr Malcolm Smith, the Countryside Council's Senior Director and Chief Scientist, commented: "Land use changes over the past 50 years have been disastrous for butterflies as their habitats have been lost to intensive agriculture and forestry... Although we have seen enormous losses, Welsh habitats continue to support a range of important butterflies and moths." That range, it seems, due to global warming, is increasing. Butterflies tend to respond quickly to changes in weather patterns and habitat and are, therefore, sensitive indicators of climate change and environmental deterioration. Higher average seasonal temperatures and milder and shorter winters have undoubtedly been responsible for an upturn in the fortunes of at least a few species of butterfly. The Essex Skipper (*Thymelicus lineola*), for instance, is extending its range and was recorded in Wales for the first time in 2000, having made it across the border into Gwent. A similar tale of expanding distribution has been recorded for the Small Skipper (*Thymelicus sylvestris*). In recent times it has colonised Powys and Snowdonia and has reached as far as the Conwy coast, and the Brimstone (*Gonepteryx rhamni*), a distinctive, bright yellow butterfly, which once was only recorded in south Wales, has recently spread westwards through Powys.

Ashworth's Rustic (*Amathes ashworthii*)

Commenting in 1890 on a species of lepidoptera unknown prior to its discovery in north Wales in the middle of the nineteenth century, Willoughby Gardiner wrote: "Who, indeed, that has seen the delicate dove colour upon the wings of this insect, when fully emerged from the pupa, can help being perpetually captivated by its quiet and unassuming beauty?" The species of moth to which the respected Victorian lepidopterist was referring to was Ashworth's Rustic, also known as 'the pride of Gwynedd'. An attractive moth, Ashworth's Rustic has a wingspan of 35–40 mm. It is somewhat variable in colouration, the forewings range from pale grey to dark slate grey with darker horizontal lines, whilst the hindwings are generally light greyish-brown shading to whitish at base. Such colouration is admirably suited to its habitats of slate and limestone hills and mountains of Penmaenmawr, Sychant Pass and Snowdon, Caernarvonshire; Llangollen, Denbighshire; and Cader Idris, Merionethshire, where it is seen in flight during the months of July and August.

It was on 20th July, 1853, when famous lepidopterist Joseph Ashworth of Bryn Hyfryd, whilst on a field trip near Llangollen, Denbighshire, on terrain he was later to describe as: "about a mile from the nearest limestone", came upon a moth that he could not readily identify. Two years later, confirmation that Ashworth's specimen was new to science came when it was named in his honour. Fellow lepidopterist Henry Doubleday wrote in *The Zoologist* : "This pretty species… was discovered at Llangollen, north Wales, by Mr Ashworth in the summer of 1853 and the specimen forwarded to me for inspection. Last summer many specimens were taken by Messrs. Cooke, Gregson &c. I have forwarded a specimen of the male and a drawing of the female to my friend M. Guenne, and he says that he believes it to be quite new. I have therefore named it after its discoverer."

A procession of entomologists followed in the footsteps of Ashworth, many combining a holiday in north Wales with efforts to obtain as many specimens of *Amathes ashworthii* as possible. In 1881, a Yorkshire collector named G. T. Porritt reported success in locating batches of eggs of the moth near Penmaenmawr and, in 1907, members of the Manchester Entomological Society recorded collecting no less than 102 larvae of the species from the same area. The attraction of adding a specimen of the moth to their collections proved irresistible to many collectors, despite the hazards such as those encountered by R. Tait, who, following a collecting trip to Penmaenmawr in 1923, was to report: "… in the excitement of the chase I kept climbing upwards and nearly brought my collecting days to an untimely end. Hanging on by both hands and feet, suddenly both handholds gave way owing to the shaly nature of the rock, and I slipped down some 12 or 15 feet, just stopping by the merest bit of luck on the edge of a straight drop of 30 feet, with 100 feet of steep hillside, consisting of loose stones, below. Needless to say I have never climbed that bit of rock again. "

Thankfully, *ashworthii* managed to survive such ravages and, indeed, has been proved to be more numerous and widely distributed than was thought in the nineteenth century. For instance, in 1962 it was reported "in great numbers" below Cader Idris, and a decade later, at Llyn Cwmynach, it was found to be one of the eight dominant species of moth in the area. Certainly, reports in the last forty years seem to bear out the comments of lepidopterist A. Richardson, who said: "this species commonly believed to be more or less restricted to Llangollen and the Conway area, must have a very wide range indeed in suitable limestone localities. Ironically, recent times have seen very few records from Denbighshire, the county where it was first discovered."

High Brown Fritillary (*Argynnis adippe*)

Considered to be Wales's rarest butterfly, the High Brown Fritillary is now extinct from 94% of its former range in Britain. A large butterfly, with a wingspan of 60–67 mm, it is a species found at sunny, sheltered, woodland clearing sites where it is seen flying from late June to mid August. The upper wings are golden with rows of large black spots and the under wings are greenish-orange with rows of large silver spots outlined in black and a characteristic row of red ringed spots. Once fairly common in woodland in Wales, it is now a rapidly declining species. Current estimates suggest only fifty colonies remain in Britain, with just five in Wales, at scattered locations in Glamorgan, Pembrokeshire and Powys. Conservationists believe, that with help, the species may well recover, and they hope that a further ten colonies can become established in Wales by 2005. However, with current colonies only numbering fifty and declining in Britain, the species is considered to be in real danger of extinction.

Marsh Fritillary (*Eurodryas aurinia*)

Wales is one of the strongholds in Europe for the beautiful Marsh Fritillary. In appearance, the distinctive butterfly, with a wingspan of 30–46 mm, has upper wings of reddish-orange with yellow-ochre patches and black veins, the under wings are considerably duller. Its habitat in the principality is open grassland and wetland sites, where its larval food is Devil's Bit Scabious (*Succisa pratensis*). Its decline in the last half a century, due to loss of habitat through drainage

and agricultural management, has been dramatic. From being relatively common, it disappeared from large areas of the principality, so that a 1990 survey put the number of colonies in the whole of Wales at only 111. In 1994, a colony was lost from Selar Farm in the Neath Valley when a water meadow was literally uprooted and translocated to the nearby Blaengwrach Nature Reserve. Despite assurances from the open-cast mining company responsible that the butterflies would follow, the experiment was a failure. It prompted one spokesman to declare: "It's another nail in the coffin of the nationally rare and declining species." Current estimates suggest around 188 colonies are present in Wales, mainly on the wet pastures in Pembrokeshire, Carmarthenshire and Ceredigion but also in Gwynedd and Anglesey.

Pearl-Bordered Fritillary (*Boloria euphrosyne*)

In common with many other butterfly species, the Pearl-Bordered Fritillary has undergone a dramatic decline in numbers in Wales in recent times. The upper wings of the decorated butterfly are an orange-brown with black veins and black spots that get progressively smaller as they meet the edge of the wings. The undersides are orange and yellow with silvery-white 'pearl' markings. Wingspan is 44–47 mm. A nationally scarce species of unimproved grassland and scrub, the beautiful butterfly has suffered from changes in land

usage, intensive sheep grazing, an increase in conifer plantations and a decline in woodland coppicing. In Wales, from more than seventy colonies in the 1970s, numbers have slumped and current estimates are put at just 30. The key to conservation of the species in the principality appears to be the preservation and extension of deciduous woodland and regular coppicing.

Rosy Marsh Moth *(Eugraphe subrosea)*

Almost half a century ago, a chance capture of an unidentified moth, made by an entomologist holidaying in north Wales, caught the attention of national newspapers and rocked the world of entomology. The remarkable discovery of a specimen of the Rosy Marsh Moth caused such a sensation that, despite the exact location of the find not being disclosed, lepidopterists from all over Britain converged on Wales, anxious to locate a specimen of a moth that had long been considered extinct within the British Isles. True to its name, the Rosy Marsh moth displays a striking, pale, rosy-grey colouration to its forewings. The hindwings are an ochreous yellow and the overall wingspan some 36–40 mm. The moth was first recorded in Britain around 1837, at Yaxley Fen in Huntingdonshire, by Richard Weaver. In the early 1850s, two fen areas were drained, its habitat destroyed and the moth disappeared. Early last century entomologist Richard South claimed: "This moth is exclusively English, at least it was, because now and for perhaps the last fifty years, it has been extinct…" The Rosy Marsh Moth was, it seemed, lost and gone forever from Britain. However, in 1965, a chance capture at a remote North Wales site led to the rediscovery of the species. On checking his mercury vapour light trap, entomologist Raymond Revell found a large moth that was not a species he readily recognised. Later, on his return to his Devonshire home, he decided to send the specimen to the British Museum for identification. It was with some surprise that on checking the identity of the moth, Mr D. S. Fletcher certified it as being a male Rosy Marsh Moth.

Since the moth was not regarded in general as being a visitor to Britain, speculation grew that the species may be resident somewhere in Wales. Meticulous research on possible habitats was undertaken by two entomologists, C. G. M. de Worms and J. L. Messenger. Eventually, they determined that conditions most similar to those at which the species was known to exist on mainland Europe were to be found at Borth Bog in Cardiganshire. In 1967, they travelled to Wales in search of the elusive moth. On their arrival, they met up with a fellow colleague, A. Richardson, who had previously made a number of trips to the area and assisted with information on possible site locations. Richardson greeted them with some astonishing news. He had been out with his light the previous night and had caught a moth he was immediately able to identify as a male Rosy Marsh Moth. More specimens had arrived later and, in total, seventeen examples of the insect were recorded. The first night of their search, de Worms and Messenger were successful in obtaining several specimens of the moth. The following evening, however, was to prove even more rewarding, when a total of 200 insects were found in their traps: no fewer than 37 were identified as being Rosy Marsh moths. In all, the number recorded in ten days, including Richardsons' specimens, reached a staggering total of 192. This was, indeed, an amazing number of a species of moth that had not been seen for over a hundred years and was previously believed extinct. Commenting on the status of the Rosy Marsh Moth in Britain in his *Lepidoptera of the British Islands* of 1897, C. G. Barrett wrote: "Hopes have long been cherished that it may still exist in some secluded spot." Such hopes were finally realised over a century later, when the moth, once considered "exclusively English" but today considered exclusively Welsh, was discovered on the marshlands of Wales.

Silurian (*Eriopygodes imbecilla*)

When Dr Neil Horton, Gwent's most eminent entomologist, visited a small quarry in the county during the summer of 1972, he could hardly have expected to record the appearance of a moth not previously recorded in Britain. Yet, that is exactly what happened, when a single specimen of the Silurian Moth came to Horton's mercury vapour light. In appearance the Silurian is fairly un-remarkable. The forewings are reddish brown in the male and chocolate brown in the female, whilst the hindwings are generally a dark greyish brown. Overall wingspan is around 24–27 mm. The species is widespread in Europe, being found in various locations, including the Alps, Pyrenees and many parts of Scandinavia, but it had never been recorded with any certainty in Britain.

Whilst the capture of the moth in Wales was hailed in scientific circles as a major discovery, there were some suggestions that the single specimen must have, unknown to Horton himself, been transported from mainland Europe in his car. This was hardly credible however, since neither the car nor any equipment used that night had been outside Britain. Undaunted, Horton continued his search, making many visits to both the quarry and other similar nearby sites, in an effort to certify the moth as a resident British species. The following three years proved fruitless for, despite his tireless efforts, no further sightings of the elusive moth were witnessed. Further searches were not made until 1976 and, finally, over two evenings, eleven specimens were attracted to Horton's

lamp. Later, having learned that the moths' continental counterparts had been seen on the wing during the day, Horton set out for the quarry one June afternoon. To his delight, he witnessed, in all, nine specimens of the rare moth, in flight in the hot afternoon sunshine. Remarkably, Horton reported: "Once, I had occasion to brush away a moth which was persistently flying, wings whirring, round my ear and this proved also to be an Imbecilla."

In 1995, a second colony of the moth was discovered 2 km away from the location of Horton's amazing discovery. These two sites remain the only locations in Britain for the moth. There have, however, been two single specimen records, both made in 1999, one in Abergavenny, the other over the border in Herefordshire. These sightings appear to suggest there are further colonies of the moth waiting to be found.

Welsh Clearwing (*Synathedon scoliaeformis*)

Maybe, because it is named 'Welsh', or, perhaps, because of the fact it had not been seen in Wales for over a century, the Welsh Clearwing always held a particular fascination for entomologists from the principality. Certainly, for generations, hopes had been cherished that the moth might again be found in Wales. An elusive moth, the Welsh Clearwing, true to its name, has transparent black-veined fore and hind wings. The abdomen has two yellow rings and

a distinctive chestnut tuft at the tail. It was first discovered in Britain by Joseph Ashworth, at Bryn Hyfryd, near Llangollen, Denbighshire, in 1854. It was also later recorded from Merionethshire, but in less than half a century after its initial discovery, the species had apparently disappeared from

Wales. A report from 1903 on the disappearance of the moth from the Llangollen area said: "the insect does not appear to have been taken there in recent years. No recent record from Wales has been forthcoming but chances of a rediscovery appear possible." Despite such optimism, however, no new sighting of *S. scoliaeformis* was to be made for another eighty years.

It was to be a chance discovery by lepidopterists during the summer of 1988 that was to raise hopes that the Welsh Clearwing might be reinstated as a resident Welsh species. Then, P. A. and P. M. Burnham came upon an adult moth at rest on vegetation in the Merioneth foothills of Snowdonia. Uncertain as to its exact identity, they sought clarification and soon became convinced it was a specimen of *S. scoliaeformis*. Realising the importance of the find however, it was decided that further confirmation was necessary. Accordingly, P. M. Burnham and three other eminent entomologists returned to the site in July the same year. After a search in an area that contained the preferred larval habitat of mature specimens of Downy Birch (*Betula pubescens*), characteristic emergence holes were found. With careful examination and removal of the bark, the typical reddish brown cocoon was revealed and, with it, confirmation that the Welsh Clearwing had, indeed, been rediscovered in Wales after a gap of more than a century. Renowned lepidopterist B. R. Baker, in his *Moths and Butterflies of Great Britain and Ireland* of 1985, commented: "There is no recent record… from Wales, but systematic fieldwork should lead to the rediscovery of this species in the country whose name it bears." Few could have realised at the time how prophetic such words were to prove for, within three years, the Welsh Clearwing was restored to the list of native lepidoptera.

OTHER INVERTEBRATES

Although they are considerably more numerous and diverse than vertebrate fauna, invertebrates tend to be more anonymous, perhaps because they are generally smaller and less conspicuous. There are an estimated 30,000 species of invertebrate found in Britain, of which around 1,700 are considered to be under threat. In Wales, there are believed to be around 20,000 species but there are undoubtedly many still waiting to be discovered. Sadly, as many as 130 species formerly recorded in the principality are thought to have been lost to Wales during the last century.

Insects make up a large part of the invertebrate fauna of Wales and the principality can claim some extreme rarities. *Porrhomma rosenhaueri*, a Red Data Book species of cave-dwelling spider, is found in two locations in Wales, at Nant y Glais Caves, near Merthyr, and Lesser Garth Cave, near Cardiff, and nowhere else in Britain. The rare Black Bog Ant (*Formica candida*) is found at only two sites in Wales, Cors Goch Llanllwch, Carmarthenshire, and the Gower Peninsula. And the most important site in Britain for the Shrill Carder Bee (*Bombus sylvarum*) is at Castlemartin Range although it is also found in Wales on the Gwent Levels at Newport, Kenfig Dunes, Margam Moors and Parc Slip Nature Reserve. The curious Mole Cricket (*Gryllotalpa gryllotalpa*) was thought to be extinct in Britain by the 1980s, but a report from 1996 seems to suggest it may still exist on the Gower Peninsula. Other Welsh invertebrate highlights include *Chlaenius tristis*, a ground beetle confined in Britain to Cors Geirch and the Hornet Robberfly (*Asilus crabroniformis*), found at scattered locations in south and west Wales. One of the most endangered freshwater invertebrates is the White Clawed Crayfish (*Austropotamobius pallipes*). A 2000 survey revealed that 72% of sites previously having the species had lost their populations. The most important Welsh sites are found on the Rivers Usk and Wye but even here numbers are continuing to decline. Although marine invertebrate fauna is undoubtedly under-recorded, the Welsh coastline is known to be home to many natural treasures such as the rare anemone, the Glaucous Pimplet (*Anthopleura thallia*). A 2002 record from Broadhaven South was the first for Wales since 1960, when it was seen at Skokholm Island.

Freshwater Pearl Mussel (*Margaritifera margaritifera*)

Once widespread and plentiful in Wales but now an endangered species, the Freshwater Pearl Mussel is a bi-valve mollusc found in fast flowing rivers and streams. The growth rate of the species is slow, taking around twelve years to reach full maturity. The life span, though, can be anything up to 120 years. Known in Welsh as *Cragen y Diluw*, the mollusc has a variable shaped shell but it is generally long, oval, blackish in colour, measuring 80–160 mm long. Its diet consists of microscopic plants and animals. For centuries the mussel was collected commercially at fisheries on the Conwy, Cleddau, Dee, Taf, Teifi, Wye and Usk. Generally, pearls from the principality were paler and although less lustrous than oriental ones, were sought-after for their varying shades of whites, pinks, greys and blues. The Romans certainly knew about Welsh pearls; indeed, it is believed that the Roman camp was situated at Caer Rhun because of the close proximity of the nearby Conwy pearl fisheries. During its heyday, pearl fishing was considered an important industry in Conwy. Samuel Lewis, in his *Topographical Dictionary of Wales* of 1883, reported that forty people were employed locally in the industry and the output was about 160 ounces of pearls per week. However, by the beginning of the twentieth century, the pearl fishing industry was in terminal decline. The industrial revolution with its inherent pollution had spelt the beginning of the end for Welsh pearl fishing.

The species is notoriously sensitive to aquatic pollution, and industrial effluents and acid rain took their toll of populations in the principality. Today, because of nutrient enrichment and river acidification, the mussel is close to extinction in Wales. Small populations are known to exist on the Rivers Cleddau, Dee, Dwyfach and Wye and although a few other rivers contain scattered individuals, these will eventually die out. On the Usk, Teme, Vyrnwy and Owen, the species has disappeared altogether, and, in 1997, a population of more than 5,000 was destroyed on the Afon Ddu by land drainage work. The only sustainable colony in the principality now appears to be on the Afon Eden, a tributary of the Afon Mawddach in Gwynedd. However, even there numbers are relatively small, perhaps amounting to less than 1,500 individuals.

Glutinous Snail (*Myxas glutinosa*)

An extremely rare and globally endangered species, the Glutinous Snail is a pond snail that occurs in clear, hard water, free from fine sediment and nitrate and phosphate pollution. Growing to a size of 15 mm, it has a distinctive glutinous mantle that covers its thin, almost transparent shell. Regarded as being plentiful in Llyn Tegid in the nineteenth century, it was recorded there up until 1953. Subsequently, two surveys in the 1960s and one in the 1980s failed to reveal any specimens. It was concluded that factors such as the lowering of water levels and, possibly, the deterioration of water quality had resulted in the snail becoming extinct at Bala. However, in 1998, after a gap of 45 years, it was again recorded from its sole Welsh site. A search for it was commissioned and on the first visit the snail was found: "…in good numbers around the edge of the lake. Indeed, the Glutinous Snail proved to be one of the most abundant snail species recorded."

Medicinal Leech *(Hirudo medicinalis)*

There are fourteen species of freshwater leech found in Britain, of which the medicinal leech is the largest. Olive greenish in colour, with longitudinal red stripes and irregular black markings, it measures approximately 5 cm long when contracted, but can extend to 12–14 cm. Individuals have five pairs of simple eyes and both male and female sex organs. It feeds exclusively on blood, piercing the skin of its host with three sets of jaws and taking up to five times its own body weight in one meal, which can sustain it for many months afterwards.

The practice of blood letting became widespread in Europe around the seventeenth century, when medical practitioners had extraordinary faith in the creature, believing it capable of drawing off 'bad blood' and thus curing a whole catalogue of complaints. In the early nineteenth century, so great was the demand for the creature that collecting from the wild became a profitable venture. Gatherers would ply their trade by simply walking around in leech-infested waters and allowing the creatures to attach themselves to their bare legs. In Wales, one of the most important sites for collection of the creatures was at Marloes Mere in Pembrokeshire.

There, it is recorded: "the waters were stirred up, the leeches netted as they came to the surface and sent to Harley Street in London." By the end of the nineteenth century, wild stocks of the creature had become grossly over-exploited. In Britain, it was declared

extinct by 1910 but later a few isolated sites were discovered, one of which was at a lake near Beaumaris on Anglesey. Although wholesale collecting had been the main cause of decline, destruction of freshwater pool and marshland habitat and a decline in populations of amphibian hosts have been contributing factors in bringing it to the edge of extinction. In Wales, a colony is known to exist at Kenfig Pool, near Port Talbot, and, as recently as 1978, the species was 'rediscovered' at Cors Goch Nature Reserve, Llanbedrgoch, on Anglesey. Ynys Môn is, indeed, the stronghold of the species in Wales, with Cors Goch being one of four sites on the island.

Snowdon Beetle (*Chrysolina cerealis*)

A very striking insect with its colouration of a brilliant fiery red or copper shot with bands of purple edged with golden green, the Rainbow Leaf Beetle is somewhat aptly named. First recorded in Wales early in the nineteenth century, its British range is confined to two sites on Cwm Idwal and four on Snowdon. Because of the latter locations, *C. cerealis* has also come to be known as the Snowdon Beetle. In 1989, the Institute of Terrestrial Ecology Research Unit in Bangor undertook a study on the life cycle and behaviour of the beetle. It discovered a strange characteristic of Welsh beetles, not consistent with individuals on mainland Europe: that their sole food is Wild Thyme (*Thymus drucei*). It also concluded that, taking into account the reliability of early Welsh records, the British population on Snowdon is unlikely to have been introduced but is probably a remnant from the last Ice Age. An estimate of the entire British population put numbers at around 1,000 adults. This contrasts with nineteenth century estimates. For instance, one report from 1856 described the beetle as: "… plentiful in Wales this season". Similarly, coleopterists Donisthorpe and Beare located two dozen specimens with ease during a cursory count in 1906. Although numbers have probably declined from those in the early part of the last century, today this beautiful little beetle seems to be holding its own. The only threat appears to be from livestock who graze the grass on which the female beetle lays it eggs.

Southern Damselfly (*Coenagrion mercuriale*)

The Southern Damselfly is a small, graceful insect, measuring just 30 mm in length, with a wingspan of 35 mm. Colouration differs in the sexes, with the males' colour developing from lilac through to blue and finally black. The species takes its scientific name from the distinctive mercury marking on the male's abdomen. By contrast, the female develops from yellow through either blue or green and finally to brown. Both sexes are seen on the wing during June–August, during which time the female lays eggs on submerged aquatic vegetation. Larvae take two years to develop to the adult stage. Britain currently holds around 25% of the world population of the species but a 30% reduction in distribution has occurred since 1960. Main factors in the decline are believed to be drainage and run off of excessive nutrient enrichment from agricultural land. Wales remains a stronghold of the species, with ten sites in Glamorganshire, the Gower Peninsula, Anglesey, Pembrokeshire, and Anglesey. One station, situated in the Preseli Mountains, boasts one of the largest colonies in Britain, with several thousand individuals.

BIBLIOGRAPHY

Bolam, George, *Wildlife In Wales* (Frank Palmer, 1913)

Condry, William M., *The Natural History of Wales* (William Collins, 1981)

Condry, William M, *Wildlife My Life* (Gomer, 1995)

Corbet, G. B. & Harris, S., *Handbook of British Mammals* (Blackwell, 1991)

Countryside Council for Wales, *Action For Wildlife* (CCW, 1997)

Countryside Council for Wales, *A Living Environment For Wales* (CCW, 1999)

Ellis, R.G., *Flowering Plants of Wales* (National Museum of Wales, 1983)

Fisher, John, *Wild Flowers In Danger* (Victor Gollancz, 1987)

Giles, Nick, *Freshwater Fish of the British Isles* (Swan Hill, 1994)

Jones, David, *The Tenby Daffodil* (Tenby Museum, 1992)

Jones, David, *Barcud – Red Kite* (Gomer Press, 2002)

Jones, Dewi, *The Botanists and Guides of Snowdonia* (Gwasg Carreg Gwalch, 1996)

Hutchinson, G. & Thomas, B. A., *Welsh Ferns, Clubmosses, Quillworts & Horsetails* (National Museum of Wales, 1996)

Lockley, R.M., *The Naturalist in Wales* (David & Charles,1970)

Lovegrove, Roger, Williams, Graham & Williams, Iolo, *Birds in Wales* (T. & A. D. Poyser, 1994)

Perry, Richard, *Wildlife in Britain & Ireland* (Croon Helm, 1978)

Preston, C. D., Pearman, D. A. & Dines, T. D., *New Atlas of British & Irish Fauna* (Oxford University Press, 2002)

Rhind, Peter & Evans, David, *The Plant Life Of Snowdonia* (Gomer , 2002)

Vesey-Fitzgerald, Brian, *The Vanishing Wildlife of Britain* (McGibbon & Kee, 1969)

Woods, R. G., *Flora of Radnorshire*, N.M.W./Bentham-(Moxon Trust, 1993)

Nature In Wales,1982–7

Natur Cymru, Numbers 1–4

**Wales within your reach:
an attractive series
at attractive prices!**

Titles already published:

1. Welsh Talk
Heini Gruffudd
086243 447 5
£2.95

2. Welsh Dishes
Rhian Williams
086243 492 0
£2.95

3. Welsh Songs
Lefi Gruffudd (ed.)
086243 525 0
£3.95

4. Welsh Mountain Walks
Dafydd Andrews
086243 547 1
£3.95

5. Welsh Organic Recipes
Dave and Barbara Frost
086243 574 9
£3.95

6. Welsh Railways
Jim Green
086243 551 X
£3.95

7. Welsh Place Names
Brian Davies
086243 514 5
£3.95

8. Welsh Castles
Geraint Roberts
086243 550 1
£3.95

9. Welsh Rugby Heroes
Androw Bennett
086243 552 8
£3.95

10. Welsh National Heroes
Alun Roberts
086243 610 9
£4.95

11. Welsh Fun and Games
Ethne Jefferys
086243 627 3
£4.95

12. Welsh Jokes
Dilwyn Phillips
086243 619 2
£3.95

13. Welsh Football Heroes
Dean Hayes
086243 653 2
£3.95

Also from Y Lolfa...

BLACK MOUNTAINS
David Barnes
The recollections of a South
Wales miner – an
extraordinary tale of suffering
and survival.
0 86243 612 5
£6.95

THE DYLAN THOMAS
TRAIL
David Thomas
A guide to the West
Wales villages and pubs
where Dylan Thomas
wrote and drank.
0 86243 609 5
£6.95

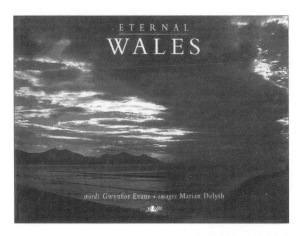

ETERNAL WALES
Gwynfor Evans & Marian Delyth
Beautiful, coffee-table book with unforgettable images of
Wales; text by Gwynfor.
0 86243 363 0
£24.95

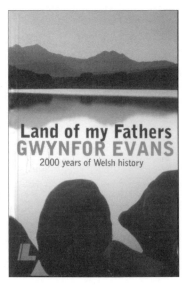

THE LAND OF MY
FATHERS
Gwynfor Evans
Lucid, masterful,
comprehensive,
passionate – and
essential history of
Wales.
0 86243 265 0
£12.95

THE WELSH LEARNER'S DICTIONARY
Heini Gruffudd

At last, a really useful and helpful dictionary for Welsh learners, with 20,000 words and phrases.
0 86243 363 0
£6.95

SOSBAN FACH
ed.Stuart Brown

Great collection of 30 rugby club songs, with music, for Saturday night!
0 86243 134 4
£4.95

For a full list of publications,
ask for your free copy of our
new Catalogue – or simply
surf into our secure website,
www.ylolfa.com,
where you may order on-line.

Talybont, Ceredigion, Cymru (Wales) SY24 5AP
ebost ylolfa@ylolfa.com
gwefan www.ylolfa.com
ffôn (01970) 832 304
ffacs 832 782